Owner-Builder
ORGANIZER

Owner-Builder
ORGANIZER

by Judy Ostrow

ALPHA

A member of Penguin Group (USA) Inc.

ALPHA BOOKS

Published by the Penguin Group

Penguin Group (USA) Inc., 375 Hudson Street, New York, New York 10014, USA

Penguin Group (Canada), 90 Eglinton Avenue East, Suite 700, Toronto, Ontario M4P 2Y3, Canada (a division of Pearson Penguin Canada Inc.)

Penguin Books Ltd., 80 Strand, London WC2R 0RL, England

Penguin Ireland, 25 St. Stephen's Green, Dublin 2, Ireland (a division of Penguin Books Ltd.)

Penguin Group (Australia), 250 Camberwell Road, Camberwell, Victoria 3124, Australia (a division of Pearson Australia Group Pty. Ltd.)

Penguin Books India Pvt. Ltd., 11 Community Centre, Panchsheel Park, New Delhi—110 017, India

Penguin Group (NZ), 67 Apollo Drive, Rosedale, North Shore, Auckland 1311, New Zealand (a division of Pearson New Zealand Ltd.)

Penguin Books (South Africa) (Pty.) Ltd., 24 Sturdee Avenue, Rosebank, Johannesburg 2196, South Africa

Penguin Books Ltd., Registered Offices: 80 Strand, London WC2R 0RL, England

Copyright © 2009 by Judy Ostrow

International Standard Book Number: 978-1-59257-777-4
Library of Congress Catalog Card Number: 2008933145

11   10   09   8   7   6   5   4   3   2   1

Interpretation of the printing code: The rightmost number of the first series of numbers is the year of the book's printing; the rightmost number of the second series of numbers is the number of the book's printing. For example, a printing code of 09-1 shows that the first printing occurred in 2009.

Printed in China

Most Alpha books are available at special quantity discounts for bulk purchases for sales promotions, premiums, fundraising, or educational use. Special books, or book excerpts, can also be created to fit specific needs.

For details, write: Special Markets, Alpha Books, 375 Hudson Street, New York, NY 10014.

Publisher: Marie Butler-Knight

Editorial Director/Acquiring Editor: Mike Sanders

Senior Managing Editor: Billy Fields

Development Editor: Lynn Northrup

Senior Production Editor: Janette Lynn

Copy Editors: Tricia Liebig/Teresa Elsey

Senior Designer: William Thomas

Indexer: Tonya Heard

Proofreader: John Etchison

To my great-grandfather William Pearson Jessup,
whose legacy as a master builder inspired an interest
that has lasted for generations, and continues.

Contents at a Glance

Appendixes

Contents

Appendixes

Introduction

When you build a house, you've committed to a project that involves a large investment of time, effort, and money. Keeping this very complex process organized and on track is a challenge for anyone, even the most experienced professional builder.

A built-to-order house of average size (these days, about 2,300 to 2,500 square feet), with good-quality features and finish level, takes at least six months to complete, often longer. Getting this job done will require a small army of subcontractors, hundreds of parts, and more decisions than you could ever count.

As an owner who's decided to contract and oversee the building of your house, possibly for the first time, you'd probably like some help identifying these details and getting them into a manageable sequence. To do this big job well, you've got to get organized.

That's the basis for the *Owner-Builder Organizer*. It's designed to help owner-builders keep their project's many steps and details together, so that they can keep moving toward completion.

How to Use This Organizer

Just as your homebuilding project is a sequence of many steps, the book is divided into a sequence of sections, each representing a phase of the process.

Part 1, "Planning," will assist you in planning your project, and includes all the necessary elements to prepare you for the actual construction of your home.

Part 2, "Construction," is a detailed outline of construction itself, from the pre-building details to the punch list and the final coat of paint.

Three appendixes offer more resources: a dictionary of common terms used in planning and construction; a list of resources owner-builders can use to further their knowledge and confidence; and finally, a few helpful lists and tables that answer basic building questions.

The organizer is light and compact, so you can carry it with you and use it every day. Inside, it's full of valuable information and tips to make the process run more smoothly, helpful lists and worksheets for the details of your project, and a Contact Lists section for your important names and numbers. It's got pockets, front and back, to store the receipts and records you acquire (and create) throughout the process, giving you a place for those slips of paper until they get back to your master filing system. *Owner-Builder Organizer* is your personal assistant for the duration of your project.

Extras

A custom-built house is like a custom suit: it's made to order. And just as each home is one-of-a-kind, by design, the experience of each owner-builder is unique. This organizer features tips and anecdotes from a number of owner-builders and building pros. Instead of one perspective—the author's—you'll have more than a dozen ways of looking at the process.

A crew of experts—owner-builder-general contractors, subcontractors from various trades, architects, and other informed sources—gives this book the added value of years of experience in every aspect of building a house. Their experiences and helpful comments are included throughout the book.

You'll also find three types of helpful sidebars in every section:

From the Home Team

Check these boxes for tips and advice from owner-builders.

Pro Know-How

These boxes feature pointers from building professionals.

Keep in Mind

In these boxes you'll find general information, cautions, and tips to help make your project go more smoothly.

Acknowledgments

As the contents of this book will reveal, it takes a village-sized group to plan and build a house. Likewise, good advice for this organizer did not come from just a single source. I am extremely grateful to the owner-builders, contractors, architects, designers, and other homeowners and building professionals, named and unnamed, who gave me big ideas, sage advice, and small, detailed tips for this book. Their experiences taught me many things I needed to know, and I hope that in sharing these experiences, you, the reader, will have an easier time with what will probably be the biggest project of your lifetime.

My thanks to all who are quoted or mentioned in this book. Many of these individuals have lives that include the role of owner-builder *and* a job in a building profession. I am grateful to you for your time and willingness to share: Stephen Beili, Cynde Clark, Jack and Andrea Donnelly, Patti Garbeck, Betsy Hagerty and Tom McNamara, Doug and Connie Hamel, Lisa Hawkins, Sheri Koones, Bill Lardi and Amy Traversa, Lizabeth Moniz and Skip Dewhirst, Mac Rood, Steve Sferra, John Terenzi and Siobhan Daggett-Terenzi, and Stephanie Wilder.

This book has lots of small details: drawings and symbols, checklists and worksheets. It required many hands to get the pieces right. My thanks to all who helped editorially and artistically: Mike Sanders, Lynn Northrup, Janette Lynn, Tricia Liebig, and Teresa Elsey at the production and wordsmith end of things; Architect Rick Thompson; Tom Schmelter of Home Designing Service, Ltd.; and artist Karen Burgess for just the right illustrations.

I salute the owner-builders among us; you are brave souls and visionaries. I wish you fine weather, great tradespeople, and the satisfaction of a beautiful house that you love.

Trademarks

All terms mentioned in this book that are known to be or are suspected of being trademarks or service marks have been appropriately capitalized. Alpha Books and Penguin Group (USA) Inc. cannot attest to the accuracy of this information. Use of a term in this book should not be regarded as affecting the validity of any trademark or service mark.

Contact Lists

As you hire members of your own Home Team, enter their vital information in this section. Use the following Quick Reference List (name and primary phone number) and the Master List (with additional space for numbers, addresses, and e-mail) for everyone involved.

Quick Reference List

	Job Description	Name	Phone
☐	Architect/Designer		
☐	Attorney		
☐	A/V Company		
☐	Bank Loan/Officer		
☐	Blasting Crew		
☐	Board of Health/Septic		
☐	Carpenter/Finish		
☐	Carpenter/Framer		
☐	Carting/Containers		
☐	Countertop Installer		
☐	Designer/Interior		
☐	Designer/Kitchen/Bath		
☐	Designer/Landscape		
☐	Drywall Hanger		
☐	Drywall Taper		
☐	Electrician		
☐	Engineer/Architectural		
☐	Excavator		
☐	Foundation		

Job Description	Name	Phone
☐ HVAC	_____	_____
☐ Inspector/Bank	_____	_____
☐ Inspector/Building	_____	_____
☐ Inspector/Electrical	_____	_____
☐ Inspector/Home (private)	_____	_____
☐ Inspector/Plumbing	_____	_____
☐ Installer/Cabinets	_____	_____
☐ Installer/Central Vac.	_____	_____
☐ Installer/Hardwood Flr.	_____	_____
☐ Installer/Siding	_____	_____
☐ Installer/Stone	_____	_____
☐ Installer/Tile	_____	_____
☐ Insulation	_____	_____
☐ Insurance Agent	_____	_____
☐ Landscaper	_____	_____
☐ Mason	_____	_____
☐ Moving Co.	_____	_____
☐ Nurseryman	_____	_____
☐ Painter	_____	_____
☐ Paver (Driveway, Parking)	_____	_____
☐ Plumber	_____	_____
☐ Real Estate Agent	_____	_____
☐ Roofer	_____	_____
☐ Sanitary (Port-O-John)	_____	_____
☐ Septic Installer	_____	_____
☐ Supplier/Lumber	_____	_____
☐ Supplier/Stone	_____	_____
☐ Supplier/Tile	_____	_____
☐ Supplier/_____	_____	_____
☐ Surveyor	_____	_____
☐ Telephone	_____	_____

Job Description	Name	Phone
☐ Utility/Electric		
☐ Utility/Gas		
☐ Well Driller		
☐ _____		
☐ _____		
☐ _____		

Government/Regulating Board Contacts

Some of these organizations impact your project; others, like schools or the post office, are good to have handy at the job site.

☐ Building Dept.		
☐ Highway Dept.		
☐ Planning Board		
☐ Zoning Board		
☐ Historic/Landmark Board		
☐ Water Board		
☐ Post Office		
☐ Local School		
☐ Local School		
☐ _____		
☐ _____		
☐ _____		

Master List

Enter complete information for each contact.

Job _____

Name _____

Company _____

Address _____

_____

Phone _____ Best call time _____

Cell _____ Best call time _____

Fax _____ E-mail _____

Notes _____

_____

Job _____

Name _____

Company _____

Address _____

_____

Phone _____ Best call time _____

Cell _____ Best call time _____

Fax _____ E-mail _____

Notes _____

_____

Job _____

Name _____

Company _____

Address _____

_____

Phone _____ Best call time _____

Cell _____ Best call time _____

Fax _____ E-mail _____

Notes _____

_____

Job _____

Name _____

Company _____

Address _____

_____

Phone _____ Best call time _____

Cell _____ Best call time _____

Fax _____ E-mail _____

Notes _____

_____

Job _____

Name _____

Company _____

Address _____

_____

Phone _____ Best call time _____

Cell _____ Best call time _____

Fax _____ E-mail _____

Notes _____

_____

Job _____

Name _____

Company _____

Address _____

_____

Phone _____ Best call time _____

Cell _____ Best call time _____

Fax _____ E-mail _____

Notes _____

_____

Job _____

Name _____

Company _____

Address _____

_____

Phone _____ Best call time _____

Cell _____ Best call time _____

Fax _____ E-mail _____

Notes _____

_____

Job _____

Name _____

Company _____

Address _____

_____

Phone _____ Best call time _____

Cell _____ Best call time _____

Fax _____ E-mail _____

Notes _____

_____

Job _____

Name _____

Company _____

Address _____

_____

Phone _____   Best call time _____

Cell _____   Best call time _____

Fax _____   E-mail _____

Notes _____

_____

Job _____

Name _____

Company _____

Address _____

_____

Phone _____   Best call time _____

Cell _____   Best call time _____

Fax _____   E-mail _____

Notes _____

_____

Job _____

Name _____

Company _____

Address _____

_____

Phone _____   Best call time _____

Cell _____   Best call time _____

Fax _____   E-mail _____

Notes _____

_____

Job _____

Name _____

Company _____

Address _____

_____

Phone _____ Best call time _____

Cell _____ Best call time _____

Fax _____ E-mail _____

Notes _____

_____

Job _____

Name _____

Company _____

Address _____

_____

Phone _____ Best call time _____

Cell _____ Best call time _____

Fax _____ E-mail _____

Notes _____

_____

Job _____

Name _____

Company _____

Address _____

_____

Phone _____ Best call time _____

Cell _____ Best call time _____

Fax _____ E-mail _____

Notes _____

_____

Job _____

Name _____

Company _____

Address _____

_____

Phone _____ Best call time _____

Cell _____ Best call time _____

Fax _____ E-mail _____

Notes _____

_____

Job _____

Name _____

Company _____

Address _____

_____

Phone _____ Best call time _____

Cell _____ Best call time _____

Fax _____ E-mail _____

Notes _____

_____

Job _____

Name _____

Company _____

Address _____

_____

Phone _____ Best call time _____

Cell _____ Best call time _____

Fax _____ E-mail _____

Notes _____

_____

Job   _____

Name   _____

Company   _____

Address   _____

                 _____

Phone   _____   Best call time _____

Cell   _____   Best call time _____

Fax   _____   E-mail _____

Notes   _____

                 _____

Job   _____

Name   _____

Company   _____

Address   _____

                 _____

Phone   _____   Best call time _____

Cell   _____   Best call time _____

Fax   _____   E-mail _____

Notes   _____

                 _____

Job   _____

Name   _____

Company   _____

Address   _____

                 _____

Phone   _____   Best call time _____

Cell   _____   Best call time _____

Fax   _____   E-mail _____

Notes   _____

                 _____

Job _____

Name _____

Company _____

Address _____

_____

Phone _____ Best call time _____

Cell _____ Best call time _____

Fax _____ E-mail _____

Notes _____

_____

Job _____

Name _____

Company _____

Address _____

_____

Phone _____ Best call time _____

Cell _____ Best call time _____

Fax _____ E-mail _____

Notes _____

_____

Job _____

Name _____

Company _____

Address _____

_____

Phone _____ Best call time _____

Cell _____ Best call time _____

Fax _____ E-mail _____

Notes _____

_____

Notes

Part 1

Planning

The saying "haste makes waste" is true of many endeavors, but none more than building a house. Although you may be eager to get started once you have a piece of land and an idea of the shape your home will take, you should take many preparatory steps before calling the excavator to dig the foundation. Hurrying through the preliminaries will result in time and money wasted: every contractor and owner-builder will tell you that good preparation results in fewer time-consuming and expensive mistakes.

Part 1 familiarizes you with the processes that begin before construction: budget and financing, site considerations, finalizing house plans, choosing materials, finding and hiring subcontractors, choosing suppliers, paperwork, and preparing a schedule. Each section of the chapter includes lists to help your planning. If you've been thinking about this project for a while, you'll already have begun the tasks in Part 1, and you'll be able to check off some steps right away.

Unless the clock on your permits or your loan is already running, it's good to take your time with planning. Changes at this stage are much less costly than corrections after you've begun building. Designer Stephen Beili, principal in the design firm Asheville (NC) Modern, says it this way: "Money spent on planning is the best money."

Budget and Financing

1

A thorough understanding of your financial resources will help you plan for your new home. It's fine to imagine the place of your dreams, but temper your imagination with a cool assessment of what you can afford.

Although about a third of owner-builders finance their new homes with their own assets, the other two-thirds must finance all or most of the project with borrowed money. To provide financing, a bank or other lender must see evidence that …

- Your budget is comprehensive and realistic.
- You can complete the construction within the prescribed time frame and budget.
- The finished home will be assessed at sufficient value to cover your debt and to provide an equity cushion that assures them you won't walk away before you're done.

The rest of this organizer will describe all the pieces of the project that will require money.

Keep in Mind

Even if you're handy and planning to do parts of the project yourself, banks want a budget that accounts for *all* labor as paid. They want to be sure that the house will be completed. If you do the labor yourself, you'll save that budget amount a cost overrun elsewhere or not spend it at all. And if you don't do the work, you've provided for someone else to do it.

Developing a Budget

From the moment you decide to build—whether you already have a site or are still looking—you need to be working on your budget.

Of course, before you've got a plan for your house, it's hard to know how much labor and materials will be required to build it. But you can get a general budget target by gathering basic data, and then refine it as your own site and plans come into focus.

Assets

If you already own your home site, this will provide you with equity—the cash value that helps secure your construction loan. But even if you've got the site, you will need additional sources of cash while the house is being built to tide you over when subcontractors need payment and you're not yet due for a draw from your construction loan.

Check with your accountant or financial adviser that the assets you are planning to use are the right assets to draw on in your particular circumstances. Certain types of assets—retirement plans, for example—may have tax consequences or penalties attached to withdrawals.

If you are considering the value of the home you own now as an asset toward the cost of your new house, remember the following:

- The house has no cash value until it is actually sold. Ask a real estate appraiser to value it at its *quick sale value*. If you need cash, you don't want to have to come up with more than you can sell the house for.

- In most cases, if you are not selling before you build, you may draw on a substantial chunk (up to 75 or 80 percent) of the value of your existing home and obtain a home equity line of credit (HELOC). These financial instruments—many of which require that you pay interest only for a period of months or years—work similarly to construction loans; you only pay interest on the cash you actually use. If you are building a more modest house (downsizing for retirement, for example), this is one way to use the sizeable equity you've built up in an existing home without moving or taking out a construction loan.

Borrowing Power

If you don't have enough cash to build the kind of house you're planning, you must be able to borrow the difference between the cost of land and construction and the assets you have available to pay for them.

How much can you comfortably afford to borrow?

Many banks have a pre-approval process that allows borrowers to learn in advance the amount of money that the bank will loan to them. The pre-approval questions require the same information as a loan application (sometimes a bit less). As you check out financial institutions, find out your borrowing power by going through the pre-approval process.

Learn Local Real Estate Values

Anyone who moves from the center of the United States to the coasts sees marked differences in the prices of homes and land. If you are planning to build in a new place, or even planning a new home where you live now, familiarize yourself with local prices for land and for new homes.

When you look at new homes that cost your ballpark budget figure, use the developer's rule of thumb: 25 percent for land cost, 75 percent for construction. If the houses you are looking at are sized and equipped the way you imagine yours will be, divide the property's cost by four and you'll have an idea of lot cost (¼) and construction cost (¾).

Collect Cost Data

If you've got materials in mind, you can start collecting information on their *unit costs*—the price per square foot, per hundred square feet (in the case of roofing materials), or per linear or board foot (framing and finishing lumber). In Section 4, you'll find comprehensive listings of materials to think about. Collect product sheets and take notes on costs.

It's particularly important to get cost data on things you definitely want in your home. As you get closer to construction, you can be on the lookout for good deals.

If you like to shop, you will be able to save considerably. You can make comparisons and hold out for the best deals.

Pro Know-How

Architect Mac Rood, who teaches owner-builders the fine points of estimating their projects, recommends the *Means Residential Cost Data* reference book, issued annually to help you estimate costs based on average construction costs in your area. See Appendix B for more info.

The True Costs of Land and Construction

It sounds simple: buy a nice piece of land and build a house on it. But you can't just add the price of land and the cost of the labor and materials to come up with a true figure for your budget.

As you consider the financing of your new home, there are other factors to weigh.

The Cost of a Lot: Land, Plus …

You'll need water, a system to dispose of waterborne waste, and power for lights, appliances, and telecommunications. A construction-ready lot can be easily hooked up to power, water, and sewer. A building-ready rural site without municipal water and sewer has been tested for a potable water source, and has acceptable soils and location for an onsite waste system, i.e., a septic tank and field.

When you buy raw land, you have to prepare the lot for these necessities. Some property sold as raw may have limited locations for waste systems or a water well. Other undeveloped lots may require significant tree cutting or other clearing. Still others may contain wetlands or other water features that will limit your ability to build.

A cheap piece of land can become an expensive one to build on if you don't do your homework first. See Section 2 to learn more about site-related issues.

The Cost of Construction

This is just labor and materials for the house, right? Unfortunately, no. So-called invisible items required to build a house include the services and materials that create its design, permits and inspections to ensure its safety, and nonbuilding material elements that support the construction.

Here's a short list of some unseen costs:

- Appraisal
- Closing costs for construction or other loans
- Your plans, which include creation of an original design or site-specific modifications to a pre-drawn (stock) plan, plus multiple copies of construction documents and specs for the building department and subcontractors
- Building permits and bank inspections; inspection by an independent professional
- Onsite facilities for waste disposal: port-o-john and waste containers
- Fencing for security and protection of natural features (water and trees)
- Installation of temporary electrical and phone lines, as well as payment for these utilities during construction

Finally, there's Murphy's Law—the unexpected problems that cost money you didn't plan to spend. Build a contingency into your budget for these problems. A modest contingency is 10 percent; a more generous (and some would say, realistic) cushion is 20 percent of the budget.

As you read through this organizer, you will find more items to add to your budget. Thinking about your project in such a detailed way will help you create an adequate budget that fits within your means.

Preliminary Budget Numbers

Refer to Sections 3 through 6 for specific elements of your budget: plans, materials, and the labor of subcontractors and other professionals involved in building.

Start with a number that represents the amount of money you have for the project. This is either your cash available plus the amount you can borrow, or the amount of available assets (your cash or the equivalent) that you can dedicate to the project.

It will take you some time to develop realistic budget numbers. You have a lot of research to do, subs and suppliers to talk to, comparison shopping trips to make. Don't rush the process. The worst-case scenario is a half-built house you can't finish because you've run out of money. Do your homework so that you know you can afford what you want.

Keep in Mind

You may want to date each budget entry so that information can be updated if the information-gathering process takes many months. In general, costs for labor and materials rise over time.

Fill in the Total number at the top based on your estimated available budget, then gather estimates to fill in the worksheet.

When you enter a preliminary budget figure for each step of the building process— the money total—put it on the first line, next to the step. Use a calculator to determine what percentage of your total budget the figure represents. Enter this figure in the second column of the worksheet next to that same step. This will help you see whether your preliminary figures make sense. If, for example, you are spending 20 percent of your budget on appliances, you need to downscale your choices. It's not necessary to fill in this second column, but it will give you an idea of how financially realistic you are in choosing materials and labor. Then you can adjust accordingly. Hint: Use a pencil; you'll probably need to make adjustments.

Preliminary Budget Worksheet

Preliminary Budget Total _____	Estimate	% of Total

Financial

Loan fees	_____	_____
Closing costs	_____	_____
Attorney's fees	_____	_____
Interest on construction loan	_____	_____

Site-Related

Lot cost	_____	_____
Title insurance	_____	_____
Survey	_____	_____
Clearing	_____	_____
Well	_____	_____
Septic	_____	_____
Well and septic permit	_____	_____
Well testing	_____	_____
Septic testing	_____	_____

Plan-Related

Stock plans	_____	_____
Plan modifications	_____	_____
Architect fees	_____	_____
Plan sets	_____	_____
Permits	_____	_____
Zoning variances (if required)	_____	_____

Nonconstruction General Requirements

Builder's risk insurance	_____	_____
Temporary utilities:		
Water	_____	_____
Electric	_____	_____
Phone	_____	_____
Waste removal	_____	_____
Sanitary facility	_____	_____
Security	_____	_____
Equipment rental	_____	_____
Office expenses	_____	_____

Construction

Excavation	_____	_____
Footings	_____	_____
Foundation	_____	_____
Drainage	_____	_____
Pest proofing	_____	_____
Waterproofing	_____	_____
Framing	_____	_____

Windows _____ _____
Doors _____ _____
Roofing _____ _____
Masonry _____ _____
Chimney/fireplace(s) _____ _____
HVAC _____ _____
Plumbing _____ _____
Electrical _____ _____
Other mechanical: _____ _____

_____ _____ _____
_____ _____ _____
_____ _____ _____

Drywall _____ _____
Insulation _____ _____
Siding _____ _____
Painting (interior and exterior) _____ _____

Finish Work
Finish carpentry _____ _____
Interior doors/hardware _____ _____
Staircases _____ _____
Hardwood floors _____ _____
Tile _____ _____
Vinyl/linoleum _____ _____
Carpet _____ _____
Appliances _____ _____
Plumbing fixtures/fittings _____ _____
Electrical fixtures/fittings _____ _____
Furnace/heating system _____ _____
Water heater _____ _____

Exterior Structures

Garage _____ _____
Porch(es) _____ _____
Deck(s) _____ _____
Other:

_____ _____ _____
_____ _____ _____
_____ _____ _____

Landscape
Driveway/paving _____ _____
Masonry _____ _____
Fencing _____ _____
Plants/trees _____ _____

Total preliminary budget _____
Plus contingency (10–20 percent) _____
Total preliminary estimate _____

Successful Financing

Deciding to be the general contractor (GC) for your own project will raise the bar for your credentials. Not only must you pass the tests for good credit and the ability to repay your loan, you will also be scrutinized for your ability to manage a project.

Banks that make loans for residential construction need to be certain that a contractor will deliver a project on time and within budget. When a bank deals with an owner-builder using a contractor it knows, its leap of faith is much smaller than when an owner-builder proposes to contract a home construction for the first time.

Thus, even if you've got a great credit rating, don't expect every bank to be willing to loan you the sum you need to build your custom home. But if you are persistent, organized, and able to present your project professionally and confidently, you *will* find a lender.

You increase your chances of a positive result by becoming proactive. Don't wait for banks to ask you for information. Have everything detailed in this section organized and ready before you present your applications.

What's a Construction Loan?

Unlike a mortgage, which is paid over an extended period—15, 20, 30, or more years—a construction loan is a short-term loan, payable over the set time that the bank has determined is sufficient for the borrower to complete the project.

When it grants a construction loan, a bank will schedule a series of completion benchmarks at which it will pay out a certain percentage of the loan; e.g., completion of foundation, closing in, etc. This schedule of payments is called the *draw*.

When the house is complete, the bank issues its last payment upon the owner's receipt of a certificate of occupancy (C. of O.)—meaning it's legal to live in the house—and the construction loan amount can then be converted to a conventional, long-term mortgage.

The Combination Loan

To save on duplication of closing costs for a construction loan and then a mortgage, some banks will offer a *convertible* or *combination loan*. This enables the borrower to convert automatically to a mortgage after the house is complete and the C. of O. is issued. Sometimes this product will carry a higher interest rate than a construction loan followed by a mortgage; the higher rate may be offset by having just one set of closing costs.

It's best to consult with your accountant or financial advisor when you are evaluating loan terms, to figure out which product best suits you.

Prepare to Meet the Lender

Don't wait for prospective lenders to ask you for information. Prepare to present your paperwork to banks in a clear, complete, and organized way.

When you have all your papers together, you can organize them in a presentation binder. You will be prepared for any loan officer's questions, and the banks will be impressed with your professionalism.

Standard Qualifying Documents

For every lender you approach, you will have to fill out a loan application. Although the documents may look different, they all require essentially the same information:

- **Personal data.** Borrower's (and co-borrower's, if a couple is applying) name, address, age, marital status, employment history, home ownership history, and personal references.

Keep in Mind

Banks can be nosier than you think. They want to make sure there are no hidden liabilities in your financial past. If you are divorced, the bank may ask for a copy of your divorce decree.

- **Complete list of assets.** Bank accounts, certificates of deposit, stock holdings, pension holdings, property—and the amount of equity in that property—and any assets with cash value, such as insurance policies, automobiles, jewelry, and art.
- **Complete list of debts and liabilities.** Amounts owed on secured and unsecured loans, credit cards, or other personal indebtedness; ongoing liabilities such as alimony or child support payments.
- **Tax returns.** For the borrower and co-borrower, usually for the past two years, but sometimes more if a borrower has recently changed jobs.

Construction Loan-Specific Documents

Before you find a lender, you'll need to do lots of preparation. In addition to proof of your employment, assets, and credit-worthiness, you must show the lender:

- A contract to purchase land, or the deed to a lot
- Your plans and specifications for the house
- A detailed budget for labor and materials
- A proposed schedule
- A builder's risk or comparable insurance policy, or the name and address of your agent with their commitment to write a policy, including its cost

---

Keep in Mind

If you're handy, a three-dimensional model of your plans can help wow the loan officer and convince the bank that you are qualified to act as general contractor on your house. Model building is taught at many design/build schools. By cutting and pasting the elevation drawings in your construction documents to cardboard or foam core and piecing them together (the ¼-inch to one-foot scale is great for models), you can give the bank a 3-D view of the house you're building. Check out www.b4ubuild.com/faq/faq_0004. shtml for general directions.

Additional Work for Owner-Builders/General Contractors

Because you've got no track record as a contractor, you'll need to show that you understand what's involved in building a house. Be prepared with the following:

- **Written estimates from your proposed subcontractors and suppliers.** This will show that your budget isn't just pulled from thin air or from a book. It shows evidence of legwork on your part. Be sure to include a copy of the bank's release of lien documents so that the bank knows you intend to have each subcontractor verify, in writing, that they have been paid. The bank doesn't want other creditors in line for the money they've loaned to you!

- **Evidence that your proposed house compares well, qualitatively and cost-wise, with other houses in the area.** Just as a mortgage lender will estimate the value of the property you want a mortgage for, the bank's appraiser will look at your project to make sure its market value will more than cover the loan amount. With the help of a real estate pro (perhaps the agent who sold you your lot), find listings of properties comparable to the one you're planning. If their prices stack up well to the cost of the one you're building, you'll score points for good research and planning.

- **A resumé of your own qualifications to act as general contractor.** Do you manage large projects? Have you contracted home improvements for your current (or previous) home? Do you have experience with building or mechanical trade work? Do you have evidence of successfully completing such projects? Can you prove your availability at least two hours each day to supervise the home building? Make sure that all the positive answers to these questions are part of a resumé for you (and your spouse or partner, if your project is a team effort).

What to Do When a Bank Says No

If a bank says no because they do not, as a matter of policy, make construction loans to owner-builder/general contractors, find out what you need to qualify. Some banks want to see a general contractor with a professional contractor's license. In this case, you can hire a licensed contractor to consult on your project, negotiating a fee.

If you are using an architect, and your architect will agree to act as project manager, you can also use this route to get a "yes" from your bank.

Don't give up. Many owner-builders/GCs have had to try a dozen or more banks before getting a "yes." But if you are confident and have done all your research and planning, you will eventually find a willing lender.

Negotiating Loan Terms

When you received your loan application, you should have also received a list of the anticipated charges for the loan. Here are some items to look for. In some cases, you can negotiate better terms. Be sure to go over your loan agreement with your attorney before the closing. He or she can help you through the fine points.

Here are some fees and terms you may find in your construction (or mortgage) loan:

- **Interest rate.** This may be a fixed percentage, or an adjustable rate linked to some standard number, such as the *prime rate*—the interest rate banks charge their best customers.

- **Origination fee.** This can go from zero to several percentage points of the loan amount.

- **Down payment.** If you have land already, this may serve as your down payment. If the loan is also financing your land, you will most likely need to put cash up front. The percentage will vary depending on the loan amount and your own financial status.

- **Title insurance and local transfer taxes.** These can be big-ticket items. Be sure you understand their costs.

- **Updating the title.** Because many subcontractors will work on your project, the bank may demand that the title be scrutinized periodically, to make sure no liens have been placed on the property during construction. This will also cost you money.

Here are additional items you will find in the construction loan agreement:

- **A draw procedure/schedule.** When can you get money to pay the bills, and what is the procedure? Usually, the bank will list the completion benchmarks, or set a "percentage completed" for issuing checks. Additionally, the bank may require an inspector to certify that the required work has been done. This will take time (for scheduling and paperwork) and money (banks usually make you pay for the inspector).

  Be sure of a few things before you sign on the dotted line:

  1. You understand the draw schedule; if the bank uses percentages, you understand what those percentages represent.

2. You are comfortable with the inspection fees and procedure for obtaining the inspections.

3. You understand the time frame for requesting a draw and for receiving it. This can drag on if the inspector is delayed or someone at the bank drops the ball.

- **Time limit.** If your construction loan requires that the house must be built within a certain time frame—nine to eighteen months is common, depending on size, cost, and complexity—be sure you are comfortable with it. You should build in plenty of extra time for weather and other unanticipated delays.

- **Extension.** If you exceed the time limit, will the bank grant an extension of the loan term? What will the extension cost in fees and interest?

- **Dispute resolution.** What if the bank decides you're only 40 percent finished, and you think you're at 52 percent? Is there recourse for such differences of opinion? Make sure your attorney reviews this aspect of your agreement.

Notes

The Site

2

Whether you have a town or city lot or acreage in the country, how you position your home to take advantage of your land's assets is an important decision.

And the decision is not always all yours. The building inspector, local water and zoning commissions, and even the neighborhood homeowners' association may have legal authority to weigh in on the layout of your property. You need to deal with the issues they raise, *before* your house plans are finalized.

The Right Spot for Your House

Before you settle on the location of your home and access for vehicles and utility lines, you need to understand what you *may* do and work with local regulators to do it with the least possible resistance.

This means getting to know the various players in the building department, local regulations, and the key members of local regulatory boards.

It also means getting to know your land. If you're a city person moving to the country, or vice versa, you may not know exactly what you're looking at. But there are professionals who can help you inform yourself and make good choices about everything that goes on your property.

Understand (and If Necessary, Expand) Your Survey

When you bought your property, you probably also received a recent survey of the lot. If you're lucky, your survey includes the topography (an extra cost when surveys are done), and the land has its boundaries marked with stakes and orange-tape flags.

If your property includes wetlands—visible water or evidence of underground or seasonal flow—or if the boundaries are complex, with many angles in the perimeter, or steep slopes, knowing your lot lines could prove very important. A *topographical survey* and *staking* are worthwhile additions if you only got an ordinary survey (the property looks flat on the paper survey, with no markings for elevations or natural features) with your title and deed.

Depending on local regulations, flowing water, wetlands, and steep slopes can affect the spot where you site your house.

From the Home Team

Owner-builders Tom McNamara and Betsy Hagerty had no choice about their house site. Lakeshore zoning and environmental regulations restricted their new home's perimeter to the footprint of an existing bait shack later converted to a dwelling. To get permits to build and their certificate of occupancy, they saw a lot more of their surveyor than they anticipated.

"We had the lot surveyed four times," says Tom. "We had to convince a lot of local regulatory departments that our site was legal and buildable. It was a difficult process, but ultimately worth it."

Even if you bought a nice flat lot with accessible utilities and seemingly clear dimensions, knowing your lot lines can be critical if you run up against disagreements with inspectors, other local officials, or neighbors.

If you've already got the survey, having a licensed surveyor stake the perimeter is extra insurance that your project will not be derailed by boundary disputes. Just remember to add this cost to your budget.

Know What Must Fit on Your Site

In addition to a footprint for the house, you will need …

- Space for a driveway.
- Space for cars to turn around and/or park if street parking is not an option.
- A place for utility and communications lines (electrical, water, gas, phone, cable) to run to the house from the street or nearest connection point.
- Space to install a water well and septic system, usually at a distance from one another for health and safety reasons, if you do not have local water or sewer service.
- Space for additional amenities, such as a hot tub, pool, pool house, shed, guest quarters, tennis court, and so on (if you want them now or in the future).
- A spot for your lumber stack, for the subs to do their cutting and assembling, for the construction trailer (if any), for the waste container, and for the portable sanitary facility during construction.

Get to Know Your Land

You may have decided that the best place to put your house is in the middle of the nice view that sold you on the lot in the first place. This may be a big mistake.

Some owners who buy country property camp out on their land to get a feel for its features, see the light from dawn until evening, and listen to the sounds from the road, neighbors, and wildlife. It's not a bad idea, if you don't mind roughing it.

You can also consult an a landscape architect or designer. Depending on their pricing policies (check first), they may consult with you for free in hope of getting your landscape business. Or, for a fee, they may advise you on likely locations for the house, driveway, and other permanent features. They can also advise on trees, plants, and shrubs.

From the Home Team

Owner-builder Lizabeth Moniz, who bought a large parcel of Vermont land with her partner, Skip Dewhirst, thinks hiring a landscape consultant is a good idea. "If the owners have control over house and driveway placement, I think it's always good to hire someone who can walk the land with you to talk about house orientation, approach, siting on the land, parking, drainage, and many other things. The mistake that many folks make after purchasing land is to find the most beautiful spot and build right there. In fact, you should build to be able to *look* at that spot."

Meet Your CEO and Other Important Local Officials

The code enforcement officer (CEO), known in some locales as the building inspector, must make sure that your project conforms to all local building codes and zoning requirements.

Before you start your project, call his (or her) office, and make an appointment to introduce yourself, and discuss your property and your plans.

In most cases, the inspector or CEO will know if part of your property is in a wetland or if it's part of a historic district. And he can steer you to the governing bodies that will hold sway over what you do on your property.

If your town has no official to supervise local residential construction, you should check in at your town office and find out what regulations apply to building, and who's in charge of enforcement. Some counties and states have regulations regarding water and other environmental concerns. You must find out before you build that your project will be legal. When it comes to building regulations, ignorance is not innocence.

Learn the Local Rules

Although many rural areas have very limited restrictions on what can be built, or where the building must be placed, most municipalities have some basic rules:

■ *Setbacks* are the distances from lot lines beyond which a house footprint may not extend. You can learn the setback requirements from the building department in your locality. If you have flowing water, wetlands, or other environmentally sensitive or significant natural features on your property, setback rules may prevent you from building within a certain distance of them. Often these rules prohibit disturbing the soil or cutting back trees or other growth in sensitive areas. Violating these environmental requirements—which often involve state or even federal regulations—can result in heavy fines and a legal nightmare.

■ Because of the trend toward larger houses—often placed on very small lots—many towns now limit the *lot coverage* of a building's footprint. The formulas, usually a percentage of the lot's buildable area, differ according to local laws, so check with the building department. Coverage may include driveways, parking areas, accessory buildings such as garages and sheds, and amenities such as pools or hot tubs.

■ If you can't build out, can you build up? Not necessarily. If your great view is shared by neighboring lots, or if your property is in a neighborhood of historic homes or one- or two-story houses, a tall house profile may be subject to *height restrictions*. Often, localities that have lot coverage and deep setback requirements also have height restrictions.

■ Some towns designate specific parts of the local landscape as *landmark features*. In my town, the stone fences built in pre-Revolutionary times are historic landmarks, and may not be disturbed without a permit. Check your locale's historic ordinances; they may affect you.

■ If you've bought a lot in a development, read the fine print of the *homeowners' association agreement*. You and your attorney should check the agreement before you purchase so you are familiar with the terms of ownership in a private or semi-private community that may have its own quirky rules. Scrutinize requirements for house placement, size, accessory buildings or amenities, even exterior finishes. They may limit the possible locations for your house, as well as its design or appearance. Clotheslines, fences, and other features may be unacceptable to the association or to its *design committee*, a group of homeowners and/or developers' representatives who will pass judgment on your plans.

Orient Your House with Green Principles

Positioning and building your house for optimum energy efficiency is no longer a frill or just a trend. With the cost of fuel increasing steadily, every choice you make about your house, starting with how it sits on your lot, can save money over the years that you own it and lessen its impact on the environment.

Here are some principles to think about:

- Work with the sun. Ideally, you want to maximize the sun's effect on your home's temperature in the winter, when it can cut use of fossil fuel. In the summer, you want to keep solar gain to a minimum.

- In the Northern Hemisphere, surfaces facing south receive sun all year long. If you want to capture solar warmth in the winter, your home's longest side should face south and have the most windows. To shelter this side of the house from the summer's heat, leave mature deciduous trees in place, or plant some. Or you can shade south-facing windows with overhangs or awnings.

- Surfaces facing north are shaded year-round. In colder climates, concentrate insulation and minimize openings on this side. This means installing smaller and fewer windows on the north side.

Preserve energy-conserving and attractive natural features:

- Try not to cut large deciduous trees on the south side of the house. They will cool and shelter the house from summer sun; in cold months, the bare trees will admit light and warmth to south-facing windows.

- If conifers stop prevailing winter winds, leave them in place for a natural windbreak.

- The natural topography of the land and interesting rock outcroppings can lend interest to your property. Because many people like flat lots, developers are often quite aggressive with the bulldozer, but there is no need to flatten everything.

Keep in Mind

Spare that tree! Tree roots are vulnerable to soil compaction by heavy construction equipment. Large trucks and waste containers parked under trees can stress trees enough to kill them. If you plan to save certain trees on your property, protect their roots by fencing off a ground area equal to or greater than the circumference of the crown—the full area it shades—with bright orange polypropylene fencing. See Appendix B for a website providing more information about saving trees.

Preparing Raw Land

If you have municipal water and sewer systems to which you can link, or have bought property with a well and septic tank and field already installed, you can skip this section. If you have raw land without a water or waste system in place, this cost should be part of your budget.

Well, Well: Locating and Accessing Water

Well drilling is work for specialists. Your Realtor, building inspector, or neighbors may have names of area drilling companies. Drilling professionals and their equipment are expensive, so reputations are important here.

Be sure to check with the local building department, water board, or other regulatory board in your area to ensure that your well site and plan conform to local regulation.

The Waste Issue: Septic Systems

If a sewer system is not accessible from your land, you will have to create your own waste disposal system, called a *septic system*, to carry waste from your home and dispose of it safely.

If you are installing septic along with a well, be sure that …

- Your plan and location conform to local regulations, usually the domain of a county Board of Health.
- Your system is sufficiently sized for your house. Septic tanks and leaching fields are generally sized according to occupancy. Thus, boards of health usually size a system according to the number of bedrooms in a house.

Keep in Mind

You may be planning a three-bedroom house, but if there is room for an addition, the next owners—or even you, a few years from now—might want to upsize. Consider installing a system approved for four bedrooms, even if you only have plans for three now and you'll be prepared for an addition in your home's future.

As you learn about the site, you may have questions or concerns for other professionals involved: the building inspector, local regulatory commissions, an architect or landscape designer. Use the Notes page at the end of this section to jot down your concerns.

Your Site Checklist

Fill in the blanks and check those items already completed. Indicate N/A for those that do not apply to your site. Then tackle the items not yet completed.

- ☐ Surveyor name and phone _____
- ☐ Landscape architect or other site consultant

  Name and phone _____

Lot Information

Lot and block number _____

Map number _____

Zoning _____

Setback requirements:

Front: _____   Rear: _____   Side: _____

Others (wetland restrictions, etc.):

_____

_____

Height restrictions? _____

Historic district? _____

Orientation Check

- ☐ House location takes advantage of solar gain
- ☐ House location is/will be sheltered from prevailing winds
- ☐ House location takes advantage of natural features
- ☐ House location preserves views

Survey Information

- ☐ Survey complete
- ☐ Lot is staked
- ☐ Property boundaries are marked
- ☐ Additional survey needed (reason): _____
- ☐ Home site located and indicated on survey

Other features on survey:

- ☐ Wetlands (if any) located
- ☐ Topography indicated (if necessary)
- ☐ Other geographic feature _____
- ☐ Other geographic feature _____
- ☐ Utility lines located
- ☐ Sewer lines located
- ☐ Water well located
- ☐ Septic tank located
- ☐ Septic field located

Other features:

- ☐ Driveway located
- ☐ Other _____
- ☐ Other _____
- ☐ Other _____

Approvals Information

- ☐ Building inspector checked survey   Approved ☐
- ☐ Building inspector checked house location   Approved ☐
- ☐ Well required   Well location approved ☐
- ☐ Septic required
- ☐ Upsize septic for _____ bedrooms
- ☐ Septic location approved
- ☐ Driveway   Curb cut needed ☐   Approved ☐

Notes

Plans

If you have land, you probably have a vision of what you want to build there. You may have enlisted the services of an architect or designer, you may have purchased pre-drawn plans, or you may have your own sketches you want to make into construction drawings. Or, if you're on top of recent buzz, you may be investigating modular home companies to prefabricate your custom home—another option for owner-builders looking for labor efficiencies and a possible shorter schedule.

This section covers things you should think about during the design phase, no matter which route you choose.

The Options

Architect-Drawn Custom Plans

Custom plans, based on ideas (yours or the architect's, or both) fitted specifically to your site, then drawn with detail sufficient to guide construction, carry the largest initial cost of four common strategies for designing a house.

An architect may be involved in one, two, several, or all the stages of the project. If you hired him or her to take part in the entire project, here's how time would be spent, on average:

1. Programming, schematic design (15 percent)
2. Design development (20 percent)
3. Construction documents (40 percent)
4. Bidding or negotiation (5 percent)
5. Construction phase (20 percent)

Architectural services usually include structural, mechanical, and electrical engineering. Consultants on these specialties are subcontractors of the architect.

Depending on the architect or firm you choose, additional services such as landscape design, permitting, and estimating may be added to the architect's duties. Depending on the nature of your contract, these will be included in the fee or contracted as needed for an hourly or flat fee.

As the owner-builder, you decide how many or how few of the architect's services you will contract for.

Choosing the Right Architect

If you have a very good idea of what you want, choose an architect whose work is similar in style and character to the design you want. Remember to pick someone who will listen to you and respond to your specific needs and wishes. The right "fit" is important.

From the Home Team

Owner-builders Jack and Andrea Donnelly found a high-profile architect with a big re-sumé and splashy portfolio (and a price tag to match). But the problems began early on. "He didn't listen to us," says Andrea, "and we wound up firing him, and losing the hefty retainer we paid him."

The Donnellys were driving around on vacation when they saw a shingle-style house that closely resembled their own ideas. Andrea knocked on the door and the owner gra-ciously told her the name of the architect. The Donnellys used the same firm, and had a good experience with the architect, a partner to the one who drew plans for the house they had admired. "He really listened to us, and understood what we wanted. The draw-ings matched up with our vision."

The only caveat: "The firm was a few hours' drive from our site, and so he couldn't be as engaged in the construction phase as an architect close by would have been."

Architect or Designer?

Architects have years of formal training and must pass a licensing examination to use the title of architect. But not every state requires that residential plans be signed or stamped by a licensed architect.

Many experienced home designers make beautiful, buildable plans that will pass muster with the building department. In some cases, you will need an engineer to review and stamp the plans; often, the designer will include the engineer's review as part of the service.

Just know your local rules, interview the designer, check his/her references, and visit a couple of finished or in-progress projects.

Custom-Drawn Plans: Cost

There are two ways to figure cost for architectural services:

- **Hourly fee.** With this fee structure, you pay for the architect's time as it is used. There is no limit to how many hours you can spend on the design—as long as you pay for them. Many architects and owner-builders like this arrangement because it keeps both parties on top of the time factor.

■ **Percentage of construction cost.** This method bases fees on a percentage of the construction cost; 10 to 15 percent is standard for a job that includes architect participation in the five stages of plan development. Superstar architects with national reputations often command a greater percentage.

The obvious drawback of a cost-based percentage is that it provides no upper limit for the architectural fee, and gives the architect no incentive to control costs. However, if you can control both the budget and your actual spending, this arrangement can work fine.

If you are paying a percentage of cost, be sure that your contract specifies the degree of service. Will the architect work with you in all five phases of the project? If not, the percentage of costs should be negotiated according to work contracted for.

Ready-Made (Stock) Plans

You can choose a house plan from thousands that are available online, through magazines, and in dozens of books. Most of these are architect drawn.

If they meet your requirements for space and design, stock plans are fine, but they are drawn to generalized specifications and may not meet the code requirements in your region or town. For example, if you live in an earthquake- or hurricane-prone region of the country, or a place with heavy, lingering snow (think weight on the roof), structural requirements will be different than for an area without these conditions.

In many cases, your stock plans must be certified and stamped by a licensed structural engineer or architect; it will depend on local laws and codes. Check with your building department before you start working on budget estimates or hiring subcontractors. Your plans should be deemed buildable first.

So don't buy a set of stock plans because you think you will save thousands of dollars. You will most likely pay a professional to modify the plans to your location. Buy stock plans if the drawings appeal to you aesthetically, fulfill your needs and wishes, and—this is very important—can be built within your budget.

The DIY Designer: You

Even if you have carefully drawn the dimensions and features of your dream house to exact scale on graph paper, you probably do not have construction-ready drawings, which are precisely drawn and include specifications for lumber, windows, doors, and other materials.

Converting your sketches to drawings a subcontractor can read and understand is not difficult. You will need a structural engineer, architectural draftsman, or architect to redraw your sketches to meet structural and engineering requirements for your area and building codes.

Owner-builder Tom McNamara had purchased lakeside property with the dream of one day taking down the rickety cottage near the shore and replacing it with a beautiful, modestly sized Craftsman-style house. He was at the schematic drawing stage—showing an idea of form, plan, and dimensions—when he took his sketches to a timber frame company, with the idea of transforming the ideas into a post and beam home.

"What they drew for us was much too expensive for our budget, but we then took their sketches and mine to an architectural design firm that created complete construction drawings for a stick-built house that we could afford," says Tom. "The timber frame company's drawings cost us a couple of thousand [dollars], and so did the construction drawings. But we wound up with workable plans that got us through the very rigorous process of building on our restricted footprint and getting the job done at a price we could afford. Really thinking about the plan and making sketches over a prolonged period helped make the design process easier, because we had a clearer vision of what we wanted."

A New Option: The Custom Modular Home

Say "modular," and many people will think of the trailer park homes that they see moving on flatbed trucks. This is not their idea of a custom home.

However, many beautiful, complex designs are now factory-built in modules that are joined together at the client's site on a prepared foundation. The closing-in process that takes a few weeks when a house is built onsite takes a couple of *days*.

If you choose the modular option, you will still need to build a home that conforms to local codes, have the slab or foundation prepared for the modules, and do the interior and exterior finish work not completed at the factory. But this option has become increasingly attractive to owner-builders who want a shorter schedule and like the efficiencies of factory-built.

There are now dozens of companies who do this type of construction. See Appendix B for more information on modulars.

Construction Drawings: Building-Ready Plans

Traditional blueprints—white lines on a special blue paper—have gone the way of the horse and buggy. Many construction drawings are now made using CAD (computer assisted drawing) software and computer printed. Some architects still do their own drawings; keep in mind, however, that hand-drawn plans must be re-drawn when any significant changes are made—a consideration if you're paying an architect on an hourly basis.

The Sheets: What's in a Set of Construction Documents?

Construction documents consist of five to several dozen *sheets*, which are single pages showing the project in various dimensions, with detail drawings for more complex parts. Some sheets will include specific instructions and schedules of components such as windows and doors. Some architects will include precise specifications for materials used in construction and specific directions for particular steps. They may also include keys for architectural symbols and abbreviations. This section shows samples of various sheets in a set of construction drawings.

Note that all illustrations of construction documents in this book are copyrighted by the architect or firm that drew them. They are used here by permission. It is illegal to duplicate such plans, which are the property of the designer.

Scale

Many residential plans are drawn to a scale of ¼-inch to 1 foot. However, various scales may be used. The survey in the figure is drawn to a scale of 1 inch = 10 feet. Some detail drawings, because of their complexity, are drawn on a larger scale.

The scale will be indicated on the document, often beneath the document title, or in the lower-right corner of the page.

Survey or Site Plan

This survey, usually prepared and signed by a licensed surveyor, shows the lot lines, features (stone walls, wetlands, water, and possibly topographical characteristics), and the location of the house and any other buildings or improvements (driveway, detached garage, pool, and so on).

A *site plan* may be drawn by your architect or designer, based on the dimensions and lot lines of the official survey. It usually contains the same information.

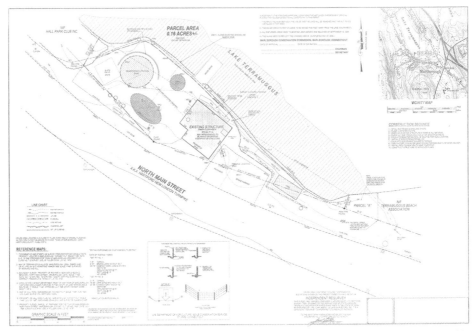

Property survey. This survey for a small lot includes a large amount of detail because the lot is nearly surrounded by a lake and wetlands, and is bordered on one long side by a road. Getting permits and approvals required four separate surveys!

Surveys must be accurate; this is why they are made by professional surveyors. Surveyors carry liability insurance in case any of the information they've guaranteed turns out to be incorrect.

Renderings

Although not necessary for construction, a perspective drawing of the house is often included, especially in the case of sets of pre-drawn, stock plans.

Exterior rendering. This drawing of the exterior of a Craftsman-style house is part of a set of stock plans. It is shown in three dimensions.

© Rick Thompson, Architect

Floor Plans

A *plan* is a drawing that shows the layout of a single level of the house. It's essentially a bird's-eye view of the structure, floor by floor. All the openings and built-in elements are shown in the plan, as are horizontal dimensions.

General crawl notes

Provide 24"x26" access door. Location as field conditions allow.

Provide foundation vents as per Local codes. Provide 6 mil film over exposed ground.

Fill piers solid with concrete. Pier block size shown is min. May vary as per foundation height.

Pier spacing may vary dependant on roof snow loading. Spacing may vary if roof is trussed.

Footing sizes are assumed - Inspectors can allow builders to adjust as long as local codes and conditions are met.

Floor plan: crawl foundation. This is a floor plan for the Craftsman-style house shown in the previous illustration. The architect has provided notes and construction details, because this is a stock plan and structural requirements may vary.

© Rick Thompson, Architect

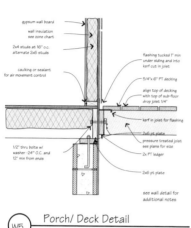

gypsum wall board
wall insulation see zone chart
2x4 studs at 16" o.c. alternate 2x6 studs
caulking or sealant for air movement control
flashing tucked 1" min under siding and into kerf cut in joist
5/4"x 6" PT decking
align top of decking with top of sub-floor drop joist 1/4"
kerf in joist for flashing
1/2" thru bolts w/ washer -24" O.C. and 12" min from ends
2x6 pt plate
pressure treated joist see plans for size
2x PT ledger
2x6 pt plate
see wall detail for additional notes

W5 **Porch/ Deck Detail**
scale 1"=1'-0"

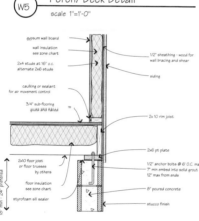

gypsum wall board
wall insulation see zone chart
2x4 studs at 16" o.c. alternate 2x6 studs
caulking or sealant for air movement control
3/4" sub-flooring glued and nailed
1/2" sheathing - wood for wall bracing and shear
siding
2x 10 rim joist
2x6 pt plate
1/2" anchor bolts @ 6' O.C. max 7" min embed into solid grout 12" max from ends
8" poured concrete
stucco finish
2x10 floor joist or floor trusses by others
floor insulation see zone chart
styrofoam sill sealer
18" min - 24" preferred

W1 **Wall detail Fl1- 8" block**
scale 1"=1'-0"

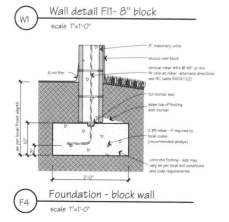

6 mil film
8" masonary units
stucco over block
vertical rebar #4's @ 48" oc min. fill cells at rebar - alternate directions see IRC table R404.1.1(2)
full mortar bed
slope top of footing with mortar
2 #5 rebar - if required by local codes (recommended always)
concrete footing - size may vary as per local soil conditions and code requirements
as per local frost depth
12"
2'-0"

F4 **Foundation - block wall**
scale 1"=1'-0"

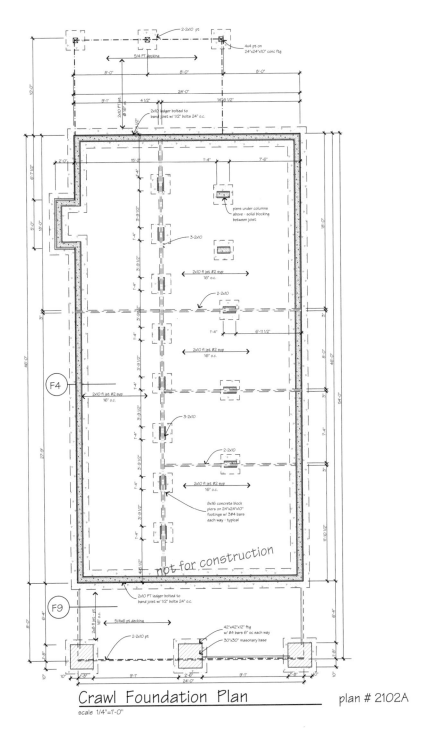

Crawl Foundation Plan

scale 1/4"=1'-0"

plan # 2102A

Floor plan: crawl foundation (cont.). This is a floor plan for the Craftsman-style house shown in the previous illustration. The architect has provided notes and construction details, because this is a stock plan and structural requirements may vary.

© *Rick Thompson, Architect*

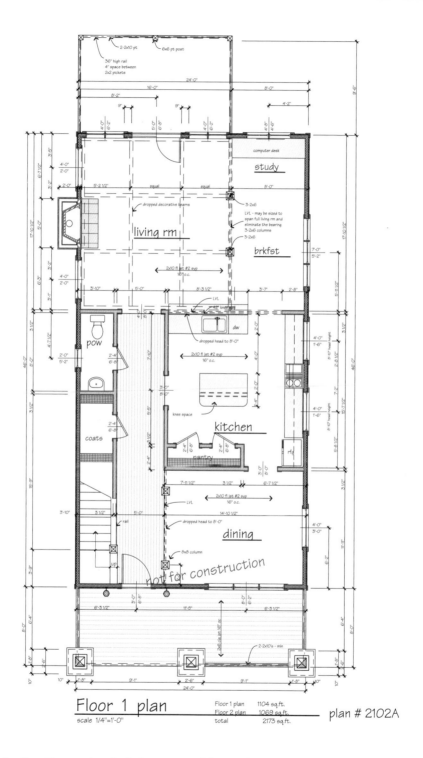

2-2x10 pt
6x6 pt post
36" high rail
4" space between
2x2 pickets

computer desk

study

dropped decorative beams

living rm

3-2x6
LVL - may be sized to
open full living rm and
eliminate the bearing
3-2x6 column
3-2x6

brkfst

equal   equal

2x10 fl jst #2 syp
16" o.c.

LVL

pow

dropped head to 8'-0"

dw

2x10 fl jst #2 syp
16" o.c.

knee space

coats

kitchen

pantry

up

rail

2x10 fl jst #2 syp
16" o.c.

LVL

dropped head to 8'-0"

dining

8x8 column

not for construction

2-2x10's - min

Floor 1 plan
scale 1/4"=1'-0"

Floor 1 plan   1104 sq.ft.
Floor 2 plan   1069 sq.ft.
total   2173 sq.ft.

plan # 2102A

Floor plan: first floor. Here are plans for the living spaces of the same house. Horizontal dimensions and the locations of all features and built-in elements are given.

© *Rick Thompson, Architect*

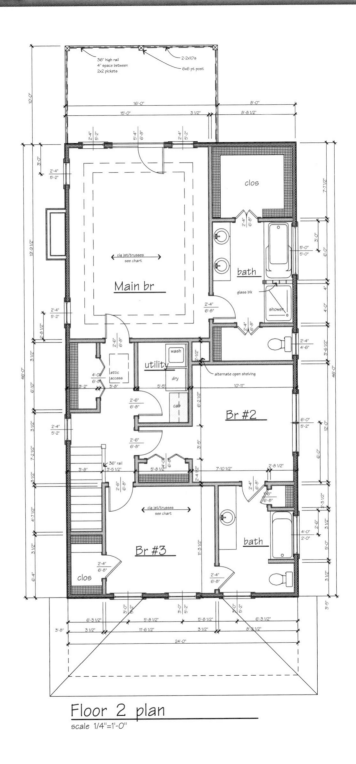

Floor 2 plan
scale 1/4"=1'-0"

Floor plan: second floor. Here are plans for the living spaces of the same house. Horizontal dimensions and the locations of all features and built-in elements are given.

© Rick Thompson, Architect

Elevations

Elevations are two-dimensional drawings of all vertical faces of the house, generally named by the direction each elevation faces (north, south, east, and west) or by the side depicted (front, rear, right side, left side).

Because elevations are drawn without perspective, they have a flattened appearance.

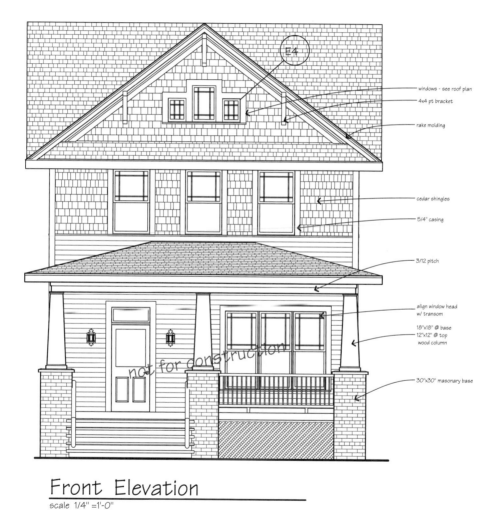

windows - see roof plan

4x4 pt bracket

rake molding

cedar shingles

5/4" casing

3/12 pitch

align window head w/ transom

18"x18" @ base
12"x12" @ top
wood column

30"x30" masonary base

E4

not for construction

Front Elevation
scale 1/4" =1'-0"

plan # 2102A

Elevation: front.

© *Rick Thompson, Architect*

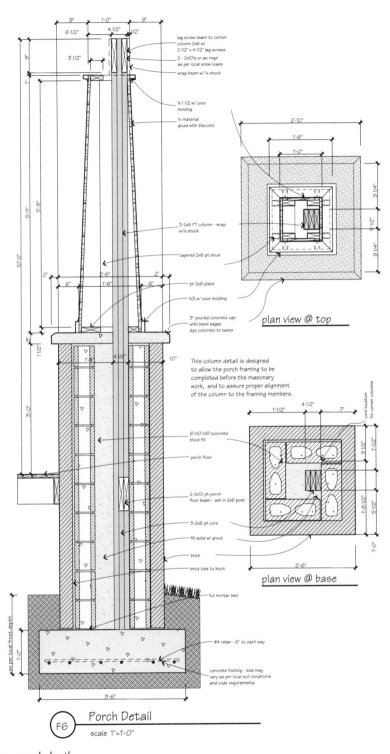

lag screw beam to center
column 2x6 w/
2 1/2" x 4 1/2" lag screws

2 - 2x10's or as reqd
as per local snow loads

wrap beam w/ 1x stock

1x 1 1/2 w/ cove
molding

1x material
glued with biscuits

3-2x6 PT column - wrap
w/1x stock

tapered 2x6 pt stud

pt 2x6 plate

1x3 w/ cove molding

3" poured concrete cap
with bevel edges
dye concrete to taste

2'-10"

1'-6"

1'-0"

9 1/4"

5 1/2"

9 1/4"

plan view @ top

This column detail is designed
to allow the porch framing to be
completed before the masonary
work, and to assure proper alignment
of the column to the framing members.

6"x10"x16"concrete
block fill

porch floor

2-2x10 pt porch
floor beam - set in 2x6 post

3-2x6 pt core

fill solid w/ grout

brick

brick ties to block

full mortar bed

core location
for corner columns

1'-1/2"   4 1/2"   7"

9 1/2"

1'-1/2"

1'-0 1/2"

5 1/2"

2'-6"

1'-0"

plan view @ base

#4 rebar - 6" oc each way

concrete footing - size may
vary as per local soil conditions
and code requirements

3'-6"

9"   1'-0"   9"

6 1/2"   4 1/2"   1 1/2"

3 1/2"

9"

9"

1"

5'-8"

5'-11"

10'-0"

2"   2'-6"   2"

6"   1'-6"   6"

3"

1 1/2"

1'-1"   4 1/2"   10"

3'-0"

as per local frost depth

1'-0"

F6   Porch Detail
scale 1"=1'-0"

Elevation: front—porch detail.

© *Rick Thompson, Architect*

50

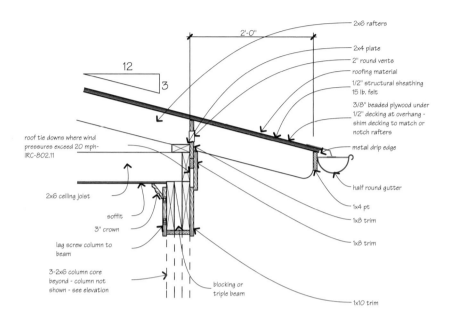

2'-0"

12
3

2x6 rafters

2x4 plate
2" round vents
roofing material
1/2" structural sheathing
15 lb. felt

3/8" beaded plywood under
1/2" decking at overhang -
shim decking to match or
notch rafters

metal drip edge

half round gutter

1x4 pt
1x8 trim

1x8 trim

1x10 trim

roof tie downs where wind
pressures exceed 20 mph-
IRC-802.11

2x6 ceiling joist

soffit

3" crown

lag screw column to
beam

3-2x6 column core
beyond - column not
shown - see elevation

blocking or
triple beam

PE1   Exposed Porch Eave

scale 1"=1'-0"

Elevation: front—eave detail.

© *Rick Thompson, Architect*

Elevation: rear. This elevation shows the house's distinctive double rear porches, one for the master bedroom, one off the living room. The expanses of window and door glass indicate that this elevation may face the home's best views or best solar gain opportunities.

© Rick Thompson, Architect

Rear Elevation
scale 1/4" = 1'-0"

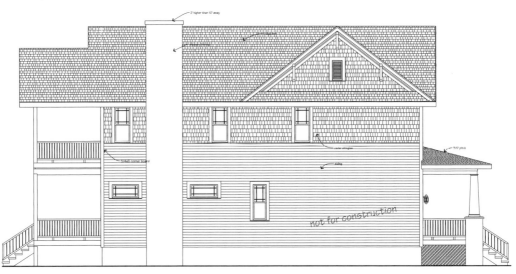

Left Side Elevation
scale 1/4" = 1'-0"

Elevation: left side. On this side of the house, you can see the decorative clerestory windows adjacent to the living room fireplace, in contrast to the simpler fenestration in the kitchen.

© Rick Thompson, Architect

Kitchen Cabinets
scale 3/8"=1'-0"

Right Side Elevation
scale 1/4" = 1'-0"

Elevations: right side exterior and kitchen. This set of drawings includes a plan for the kitchen cabinet configuration and layout, as well as the right side exterior. If you compare the elevations with the plans on the previous pages, you can see how the layouts create the configuration of the exterior openings. Note the clerestory windows in the kitchen elevation, and how they match up with the exterior right side.

© *Rick Thompson, Architect*

Sections

Imagine slicing a house vertically, from roof to basement. That's the concept of the *section*, the drawing that provides information about the building's interior vertical structure and dimensions.

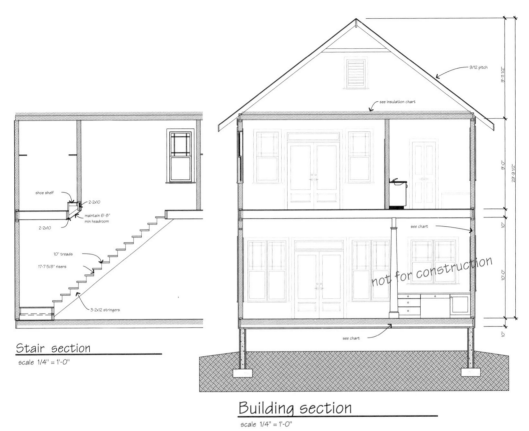

Stair section
scale 1/4" = 1'-0"

Building section
scale 1/4" = 1'-0"

Sections: building and stairs. These section drawings show such details as ceiling heights, walls, and rafters. The stair section is particularly helpful, as fitting the stairs is one of the more complicated problems of construction.

© Rick Thompson, Architect

Mechanical and Electrical Plans

If your pre-drawn or architect's original plans do not have an electrical plan, you can work out the locations of electrical controls and fixtures with your subcontractor. In fact, all the mechanicals (plumbing, HVAC, etc.) may be added later to a copy of your floor plans.

Bear in mind, however, that the locations of the mechanicals must comply with local codes. Allow time to plan your wiring and plumbing runs. The worst time to decide is when your subcontractor is standing in front of you and needs an answer *now*.

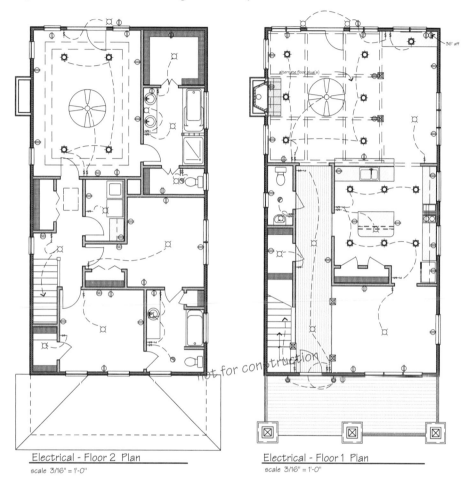

Electrical - Floor 2 Plan
scale 3/16" = 1'-0"

Electrical - Floor 1 Plan
scale 3/16" = 1'-0"

Electrical plans: first and second floors. These electrical plans were pre-drawn by the architect, not by the electrician. Note that the scale is ³⁄₁₆ inch to 1 foot, unlike the other drawings.

© *Rick Thompson, Architect*

From the Home Team

Owner-builder Siobhan Daggett-Terenzi has a knack for strategic placement of electrical receptacles. She suggests some overlooked locations:

- **Under windowsills:** If you do a lot of Christmas decorating, this is a logical place to plug in light strings and electric candles.

- **Above the mantel:** If you want illumination here, don't forget a receptacle.

- **In the middle of the floor:** If you have an open plan layout, you will want table or floor lamps in places not close to a wall. Forgo extension cords and install receptacles in strategic spots in the floor.

- **Outside:** For holiday lights and running electrical equipment outdoors, don't forget receptacles on the outside of your house. Be sure the receptacles have covers so they don't get wet when it rains. Naturally, all exterior electric work must be code-compliant.

Schedules

In some cases, architects will note *schedules* (lists) of major elements for the design, such as windows and doors.

WINDOW SCHEDULE

MODEL NO.	ROUGH OPENING	COMBINED SQ. FT. GLASS	NET CLEAR OPENING WIDTH	HEIGHT	SQ. FT. CLEAR OPENING
DHT1815	1'-10 1/8"X1'-7 7/8"	1.46			
DHT2815	2'-10 1/8"X1'-7 7/8"	2.62			
DHT3015	3'-2 1/8"X1'-7 7/8"	3.01			
TW2832	2'-10 1/8"X3'-4 7/8"	5.98	29 7/8"	16 1/4"	3.37
TW2852	2'-10 1/8"X5'-5 1/4"	11.0	29 7/8"	28 1/4"	5.68
TW3052	3'-2 1/8"X5'-5 1/4"	12.6	33 7/8"	28 1/4"	6.64
FWG 60611	6'-0"X6'-11"	24.86	28 1/8"	78 1/8"	15.28
NOTE: ALL WINDOWS ARE DESIGNATED W/ ANDERSEN MODEL NUMBERS					

Window schedule. Not just any windows would do for the water-facing side of Betsy Hagerty and Tom McNamara's house. They wanted lots of windows, in the Arts and Crafts style. The design firm that drew the house also drew up the window schedule.

© *Home Designing Service, Ltd.*

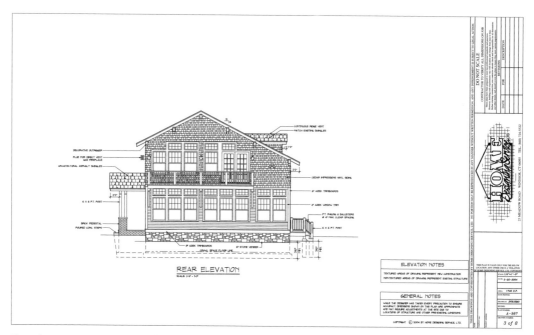

REAR ELEVATION
SCALE 1/4" = 1'0"

Rear elevation. Not just any windows would do for the water-facing side of Betsy Hagerty and Tom McNamara's house. They wanted lots of windows, in the Arts and Crafts style. The design firm that drew the house also drew up the window schedule.

© *Home Designing Service, Ltd.*

Specifications

The specs, or *specifications*, as they are formally known, are essential for good cost estimate. You want the job to be done with certain materials and techniques, and you need to specify these when contracting for the construction.

Some architects and designers will write specifications directly on the plans; others will create separate lists. If you or a nondesigner does the specifications, you must be as precise as you can about the source and grade of everything you use. If you're not, an unscrupulous person may substitute lesser materials when you're paying for better.

FRAMING SPECIFICATION

1. ALL FRAMING LUMBER SHALL BE DOUGLAS FIR OF THE FOLLOWING GRADES:
   2 X 4 STUDS- STANDARD & BETTER
   JSTS/BEAMS/2 X 6 STUDS-NO. 2 & BETTER
   #2 D.F. BASE-VALUE FB 875
   E = 1,600,000

2. APPROVED NATURALLY DURABLE OR PRESSURE PRESERVATIVELY TREATED WOOD SHALL BE USED FOR THOSE PORTIONS OF WOOD MEMBERS THAT FORM THE STRUCTURAL SUPPORTS OF BUILDINGS, BALCONIES, PORCHES OR SIMILAR PERMANENT BUILDING APPURTENANCES WHEN SUCH MEMBERS ARE EXPOSED TO THE WEATHER WITHOUT ADEQUATE PROTECTION FROM A ROOF, EAVE, OVERHANG OR OTHER COVERING THAT WOULD PREVENT MOISTURE OR WATER ACCUMULATION ON THE SURFACE OR AT JOINTS BETWEEN MEMBERS. SUCH MEMBERS SHALL INCLUDE:
   A. HORIZONTAL MEMBERS SUCH AS GIRDERS, JOISTS AND DECKING.
   B. VERTICAL MEMBERS SUCH AS POSTS, POLES AND COLUMNS.
   C. BOTH HORIZONTAL AND VERTICAL MEMBERS.

3. ALL NAILS SHALL BE HOT-DIPPED GALV. WHERE EXPOSED TO EXTERIOR.

4. DOUBLE JOISTS UNDER ALL PARTITIONS.

5. THERE SHALL BE NO NAILING INTO END GRAIN. END CONNECTORS SHALL BE MADE W/ 16 GA. GALV. MTL. CONNECTORS, JOIST HANGERS, ETC.

Framing specifications. The design firm that drew the McNamara/Hagerty house listed these specifications for framing, based on the house's structural requirements.

© *Home Designing Service, Ltd.*

Reading Plans

Construction drawings use a system of symbols and abbreviations that is a language all its own.

Often, the surveyor (for the land survey) or the designer (for the construction drawings) will provide some type of key to the graphic conventions used to identify geological, structural, and mechanical elements. The frustrating thing about these keys is that sometimes the graphic element you're trying to identify is not listed!

Also, many bits of information that the designer adds to the plans use abbreviations with which you may not be familiar. Turn to Appendix C for keys for both.

How Many Sets of Construction Documents?

If you are ordering stock plans, the best option is to first order a set of nonconstruction study plans, so that you can see if the design matches up to your site and your requirements for space and style.

Most general contractors and owner-builders need at least eight sets:

- One for you, the general contractor (GC), which will act as a working document, always at the building site
- One for the construction manager (if you are working with one)
- Two for the building inspector; one is kept on file, the other used as a working document
- Four or five sets for subcontractors for bidding, and then for major subs, such as your carpenters, electrician, HVAC, and plumbing contractors

If you are working with an architect, he or she can make as many sets as you need. If you are buying pre-drawn stock plans, you might want to invest in *reproducible* plans, so you can make extra sets.

A Change of Plans

In Section 7, we'll delve into change orders, which alter the scope of the work, the cost of your project, and the existing construction documents. These changes are made *during* construction. Because you have legal contracts with your subcontractors, changes must be made carefully, with the acceptance of all parties involved.

You cannot just red-pencil in a new change. If the change is significant, you, the contractor, and possibly the building inspector will need a visual explanation of what is altered. You may need your architect or draftsman to make a drawing of the changed element.

Once you start building, changing plans can become very expensive and time-consuming.

Plans That Fit

Plans on the Land

If you've got a small lot, the location of your house will be somewhat limited. On a bigger property, there are more options. Nonetheless, you need to decide on the locations of everything that must fit on the land: house, garage, well and septic if needed, driveway, parking area, and any other built features.

A surveyor can make sure that all the elements of your building plan fit within the necessary setbacks and property lines. Be sure that the survey cost is part of your budget.

Tweaking Your Plans

Any necessary modifications you make to plans before building are saved money later. As you go through the planning process, ask the people involved to weigh in on your plans. If they have questions, it's a good time to adjust the plans according to their concerns. On the spot, on the job, with the clock ticking and money being spent, it will be much more anxiety-provoking to make changes.

Ask for advice:

- The building inspector should see your plans after the survey is done and you think the drawings are in shape for a permit application. Ask the inspector if he or she sees any glaring problems or errors. If the house or any feature is too close to lot lines or wetlands, now's the time to make adjustments.

■ When subs are looking at the plans to prepare a bid or estimate, tell them to ask questions if the drawings give them any concerns. If you can't answer those questions, take them to the architect or the professional who certified your stock plans.

From the Home Team

North Carolina owner-builder Stephanie Wilder has a great reminder about your plans and design: "Measure all the furnishings you want to move to the new house, so you will have a place for them. Decide what you're going to part with, too, so your new house won't be cluttered with things you don't really want."

Energy Considerations and Green Features

Window selection, insulation, and even framing decisions can affect your home's energy efficiency. And there are *hundreds* of products that, when purchased instead of a standard product, can save you thousands of kilowatt-hours of electric costs, burn less fuel, and keep the air and the earth healthier.

Often you will not have to alter your design, but just change specifications for more efficient insulation, windows, doors, fixtures, and systems.

To build the best house for the planet and your pocketbook, see Appendix B for books and websites about green building and earth-friendly materials.

Design Points to Ponder

If you had it to do over again, what would you change about your plans? I asked the owner-builders who helped with this book to consider this question to inspire you to review your plans *one more time*, even if you think you've got it all just right.

Although most of the people who were interviewed for this book *love* the houses they wound up with, there's usually something they might have done better. Here are a couple of "if onlys":

"I got the beautiful, big kitchen I wanted. But since the kitchen window over the sink faces our view, I would have made it bigger."—Connie Hamel

"I would have made my utility room larger, so the equipment is easier to service, and there's more space for storage, which is in short supply in my house."—Lisa Hawkins

"I would have put another bathroom on the lower level, so that when we entertain outside, our guests don't have to walk through the guest bedroom to use that bath."—Siobhan Daggett-Terenzi

Other Details to Think About

Sometimes the holes in your design planning become apparent only as your subs are doing the finish work. The decisions at that point can seem endless and exhausting, particularly when a sub needs an immediate answer that you're not prepared to give.

Some of the details that you can decide on now:

- **The look of openings, inside and out.** Perhaps you've located your windows to frame beautiful outside views. But check the look of your exterior elevations; if the windows and doors seem a randomly placed hodgepodge of different styles on paper, they'll only look more so when built. If you need help pulling the inside and outside looks together, check with your architect or designer, or hire one to fix up your stock plans.

- **Door hardware.** Choosing doorknobs seems like a no-brainer, but even if you select off-the-shelf knobs and hinges, you still need to select the finish.

- **Window and door trim, baseboards and molding.** These decorative features can take a lot of thought, and the difference between a simple Colonial casing and elaborate crown molding can be hundreds, if not thousands of dollars.

- **The places where surfaces meet.** Generally, good finish installers will make transitions between floor or wall finishes in logical places, such as under doors. Think now: where does the tile begin and end? The stone? The hardwood? You not only need to figure how much of each material to order, but where it will be installed.

Interior Design and Decorating Help

Are you intimidated by the sheer number of choices for materials and finishes for your interior (and even exterior) surfaces and spaces?

Choosing all the wall, floor, ceiling, cabinet, fixture, and hardware finishes for a whole house adds up to dozens of decisions—probably more decorating than you've ever done before. If you're intimidated by the size of the project, you can get help.

If you're working with an architect, he or she will often have a designer on staff, or a consulting relationship with several interior designers. You can also call the local chapter of the American Society of Interior Designers (ASID) to help you locate a professional designer.

If you just need help choosing a color scheme or selecting coordinating finishes and fabrics, you can hire designers on an hourly basis.

From the Home Team

By the time she and her husband got to selecting finishes, owner-builder Betsy Hagerty was exhausted by all the decision-making. "It was time to pick colors, and I was at a loss," she recalls. "A friend referred me to an interior designer, who helped me pull together all the colors for the house. I hired her by the hour, just for the decisions I had a hard time with, so it wasn't really expensive. She saved me so much stress and aggravation; it was money well spent. I love the colors we chose!"

If you want the full-service treatment—a designer who will shop for you and guide all your decorating selections, you will have to negotiate terms—by the hour, or for a project fee. An interior designer or color consultant is a subcontractor, just like your carpenter or plumber. You should interview potential designers and get references, just as with other subs. Depending on the complexity of the job, you may need a formal contract. See Sections 5 and 7 for more information.

Your House Plans Checklist

As you prepare your plans, check off the completed elements on the following checklist.

Survey or Site Plan

☐ Survey

☐ Survey with house located

Other features located: _____

☐ Driveway

☐ Well

☐ Septic

☐ Electric line

☐ Water supply

☐ Sewer

☐ Accessory structures/other features: _____

_____

_____

_____

For Architect-Drawn Plans

Completed: _____

☐ Schematic (sketch)

☐ Design developed

☐ Construction documents

For Designer-Drawn, Ready-Made (Stock), DIY, or Modular Plans

☐ Architect/engineer signature required?   Yes ___ No ___

If yes, name of architectural drafting/engineering firm who will draw/certify plans. Enter contact info in the Contact Lists in the front of this book.

Name _____

Number of Plan Sets Needed: _____ Total

____ Self
____ Building department
____ To subs
____ Other (indicate who/how many)_____

_____

_____

_____

Construction Drawings/Documents

Plans:

☐ Foundation

☐ Framing

☐ First floor

☐ Second floor

☐ Other: _____

☐ Other: _____

☐ Other: _____

House elevations (may be front, rear, right, left, or north, south, east, west):

☐ Front

☐ Rear

☐ Right

☐ Left

Other elevations:

☐ Kitchen

☐ Other _____

☐ Other _____

Sections:

☐ _____

☐ _____

☐ _____

☐ _____

Details:

☐ _____
☐ _____
☐ _____
☐ _____

Specifications/schedules (please list):

_____
_____
_____
_____
_____

☐ Materials list

Review by Building Department

☐ Reviewed
☐ Approved

Changes/concerns (please list):

_____
_____
_____
_____
_____
_____
_____

Notes

_____
_____
_____
_____
_____
_____
_____
_____
_____
_____
_____
_____
_____
_____
_____
_____
_____
_____
_____
_____
_____
_____
_____
_____
_____
_____
_____
_____
_____

Materials

4

The cost of materials will test your budget discipline. From framing lumber, siding, and roofing, to flooring, light fixtures, and hardware, thousands of parts come together to build a home.

When you're tempted by beautiful magazine spreads and home and garden television programs that tout the latest building materials and finishes, it's hard to contain the impulse to order expensive, trendy items for your house. But unless your funds are truly unlimited, you'll have to make real choices about the right stuff to construct and finish your home.

Here's what owner-builder Cynde Clark says about her shopping:

"I wanted to stick closely to my budget, so I was careful about all my selections. I found many stylish items that I liked, but I was strict with myself about prices. First of all, I gave myself three or four choices for almost everything that 'shows,' like hardware, lighting, and appliances. My selections were similar in style and price, so it wouldn't be so wrenching if we couldn't get my first choice, for whatever reason. This kept me from having to make a hasty decision, or move up in price when something was out of stock or discontinued; I just used an alternate from my list. And to keep me honest, I also took the contractor who worked with me along on some key shopping trips. He knew what the allowances were for finishes, and helped me resist temptation."

Organizing Your Material Needs: A Master List

There are so many pieces and parts in a new house that it's incredibly easy to forget things when you're planning, only to remember them when you're over budget and behind schedule. And if you think this is a problem for you, consider the difficulties of large commercial projects, which must be built to stringent standards of safety and durability.

To address the need for a comprehensive organizing system for specifying methods and materials for commercial building projects, the Construction Specifications Institute (CSI) created the Master Spec format for organizing and categorizing used in planning, building, maintaining, and even demolishing a commercial structure.

This formatting system is extensive and covers many more items than the average house (or even the above-average house) will use. However, you can check that you've covered your bases by using this format's 16 divisions (categories of work) from the 1995 edition. If you want to be completely up to date, you can use the updated 2004 format, which has 48 divisions, many of which are reserved for future categories of materials, equipment, procedures, and other things you won't require.

If you are using an architect or designer, he or she may write specifications with numbers from the CSI divisions.

See Appendix B for more information on obtaining complete listings of both specification formats.

The following listing of the 16 divisions and their subcategories provides you with a checklist of materials that you or your subs will buy. Indicate "by sub" if you will not purchase the material.

Division 1: General Conditions

This division covers the parts of your project that do not become part of the house. But you need them to get the work done. Indicate N/A (not applicable) for those items not part of your project.

☐ Job site setup
_____ Temporary sanitary facilities
_____ Waste containers
_____ Trash removal
_____ Temporary utility setup
_____ Temporary phone hookup
_____ Trailer [for storage or meetings]
_____ Site security

☐ Administrative
_____ Mail
_____ Phone
_____ Banking
_____ Copies

☐ Miscellaneous (use this space to note any other items that are not part of tangible work on your project)

_____

_____

_____

_____

Division 2: Site Work

- ☐ Pre-cast concrete (septic system)
- ☐ Fill _____ Topsoil _____ Gravel _____
- ☐ Pipe
- ☐ Drainage tile
- ☐ Pavers
- ☐ Stone
- ☐ Fencing

    _____ Temporary fencing (to prevent storm-water runoff, protect trees, etc.)

    _____ Permanent fencing

- ☐ Other materials for site _____

    _____

    _____

    _____

Division 3: Concrete

- ☐ Forms
- ☐ Rebar
- ☐ Mesh
- ☐ Concrete
- ☐ Gunite (sprayed concrete)
- ☐ Aggregate
- ☐ Tint
- ☐ Other _____

    _____

    _____

    _____

Division 4: Masonry

- ☐ Concrete masonry units (concrete block)
- ☐ Interior and exterior brick
- ☐ Stone
- ☐ Mortar

Division 5: Metals

- ☐ Steel framing, studs, I-beams
- ☐ Railings
- ☐ Steel columns
- ☐ Radiator covers or other decorative grilles
- ☐ Fencing

Division 6: Wood and Plastics

- ☐ Dimensional lumber
- ☐ Timbers
- ☐ Pressure-treated wood
- ☐ Plywood
- ☐ Trusses
- ☐ Engineered wood
- ☐ Wainscoting, paneling
- ☐ Trim and molding
- ☐ Stair treads and trims
- ☐ Wood railings
- ☐ Stair systems
- ☐ Plastic laminates
- ☐ Wood replacement products
- ☐ Urethanes
- ☐ Synthetic solid surfacing
- ☐ Fasteners for wood and plastic materials

Division 7: Thermal and Moisture Protection

- ☐ Insulation
  - _____ Foundation, rigid board
  - _____ Batting
  - _____ Blown-in

- ☐ Barrier wrap
- ☐ Felt paper
- ☐ Plastic sheathing
- ☐ Flashing
- ☐ Waterproof membranes

☐ Roofing
_____ Shingles
_____ Tiles
_____ Slates
_____ Rolled roofing
_____ Metal

☐ Siding
_____ Clapboard
_____ Stucco
_____ Shingle
_____ Cement fiber
_____ Adobe
_____ Metal
_____ Other

☐ Sealants
_____ Caulk
_____ Foam
_____ Other

☐ Other insulating/waterproofing products _____

_____

_____

_____

_____

Division 8: Openings

You will labor over the many choices of materials, degrees of energy efficiency, and even hardware colors available for your windows, doors, and skylights.

If an architect drew your plans, he will probably make up a schedule based on the type of windows and doors you choose.

Take your time choosing openings. Windows and doors can account for 10 percent or more of your construction budget.

☐ Doors
☐ Windows
☐ Skylights

□ Hardware
_____ Hinges
_____ Knobs
_____ Locks (doors *and* windows)
_____ Window lifts
_____ Strike plates
_____ Door knockers (optional)

Keep in Mind

It's efficient to choose all the hardware for your windows and doors in a single color or metal finish. A uniform color and finish for these details gives the house a unified appearance. Remember that you'll use different types of doorknob sets, depending on the location of the door:

- *Dummy* doorknobs don't turn and are often used just for appearance.

- *Passage* doorknobs turn, but have no keys or locks; these are often used in children's bedrooms or playrooms.

- *Privacy* doorknobs lock and can be unlocked only from the inside; these are good for adult bedrooms and bathrooms.

- *Keyed entry* doorknobs mean just that; to gain entrance, you must unlock them with a key.

Division 9: Finishes

This division refers to any materials applied to rough carpentry surfaces.

□ Soundproofing
□ Drywall (also green board and blue board, which are variations)
□ Concrete board
□ Plaster
□ Veneer plaster
□ Paneling
□ Ceramic tile
□ Wallpaper
□ Paint
□ Ceilings (tin, textured, acoustic)
□ Flooring
_____ Carpet
_____ Vinyl

_____ Linoleum
_____ Tile
_____ Wood
_____ Laminate

☐ Countertops
_____ Laminate
_____ Wood
_____ Tile
_____ Stone

Division 10: Specialties

☐ Towel bars
☐ Toilet paper holders
☐ Grab bars
☐ Medicine cabinets
☐ Vents and louvers (e.g., attic vents)
☐ Fire extinguishers
☐ Pull-down stairs
☐ Mailboxes
☐ Shutters
☐ Signs
☐ Shelving (storage, closets, etc.)

Division 11: Equipment

☐ Garage door openers
☐ Kitchen appliances

_____ Range
_____ Ovens
_____ Refrigerator
_____ Dishwasher
_____ Trash compactor

☐ Laundry equipment

_____ Clothes washer
_____ Dryer

☐ Central vac system
☐ Safe

Division 12: Furnishings

This division includes cabinetry and window treatments.

- ☐ Kitchen cabinets
- ☐ Cabinet hardware
- ☐ Bathroom vanities
- ☐ Office cabinets
- ☐ Drapery hardware

Division 13: Special Construction

Any space with a specialized function fits in this category. Most use regular construction materials and specialized equipment.

- ☐ Greenhouse
- ☐ Home theater
- ☐ Wine cellar
- ☐ Darkroom
- ☐ Sauna
- ☐ Other _____

_____

_____

_____

Division 14: Conveying Systems

- ☐ Elevator
- ☐ Chair lift
- ☐ Dumbwaiter

Division 15: Mechanical

This division includes plumbing, heating, ventilation, and air-conditioning (HVAC), as well as the distribution system for these mechanicals.

Because technological advances have broadened the scope of this division, in the new specifications format (2004) Division 15 is reserved for future use; Plumbing is moved to new Division 22, and Heating, Ventilation and Air Conditioning to Division 23.

- ☐ Sinks
- ☐ Garbage disposal

- ☐ Toilets
- ☐ Showers
- ☐ Bathtubs
- ☐ Faucets
- ☐ Drains
- ☐ Pipe (supply, waste, vent)
- ☐ Fans
- ☐ Water heater
- ☐ Water filter
- ☐ Furnace
- ☐ Boiler
- ☐ Heat pump
- ☐ Duct work
- ☐ Radiant heat coil
- ☐ Dehumidifier
- ☐ Humidifier
- ☐ Air filter
- ☐ Sprinkler system
- ☐ Solar power system

Keep in Mind

Don't forget to seal ductwork and insulate pipes; you will waste much less energy when your water and air supplies don't leak hot and cold. A small investment in insulating and sealing material (and your HVAC sub's labor) will reap big rewards after you move in.

Division 16: Electrical

In the new format, Electrical is now Division 26.

- ☐ Panel box
- ☐ Cable and wire
- ☐ Light fixtures
- ☐ Receptacles
- ☐ Switches
- ☐ Dimmers
- ☐ Motion sensors

☐ Timing devices

☐ Phone and cable jacks

☐ Intercom systems

☐ Security systems

☐ Smoke, carbon monoxide, and radon detectors

☐ Thermostats

☐ Doorbells

☐ Speakers

☐ Other _____

_____

_____

_____

Keep in Mind

Your electrical system is pricey, but don't forget the covers for switches and receptacles. These range from inexpensive toggle switches and plastic covers to fancy metallic or colored enamel covers and high-tech switches and knobs.

Good Deals

The best strategies to save money on materials include some common elements:

- **Timely ordering.** When you start looking for materials, always ask: How long will it take to get an item delivered to my building site? When it's time for finishes, they need to be onsite.

- **Volume discounts.** You'll be ordering some things in significant multiples: window and door hardware, light fixtures, decorative switches, and receptacle covers. Negotiate for a "cheaper by the dozen" price break.

- **Special sales.** Often, manufacturers arrange promotions with their high-volume retailers. "Truckload sales" on big-ticket items—windows, doors, plumbing fixtures—can save you hundreds of dollars, if you know what you need and *have a place to store the material until it's time for installation.*

- **Comparison shopping.** You cannot save money when a contractor is asking you to make an ordering decision *today!* If you plan ahead for materials and supplies, you can search for the lowest price. Visit specialty outlets, and home centers and look online to find the best deals.

More Pointers from Owner-Builders

Experience is a great teacher. Here are some very helpful material shopping strategies from owner-builders:

- **Use luxury details sparingly, but strategically, for greater impact.** Owner-builder Siobhan Daggett-Terenzi used plain white tile in her master bath, but gave the pattern an eye-catching focal point with a hand-painted art tile, framed with tiny mosaic pieces, on the shower wall. The striking small detail provides style without breaking the bank. Siobhan also used a hand-painted motif on the back-splash over the range in her kitchen. Again, this focal point adds drama at low cost, because the rest of the kitchen tile is plain.

- **Set aside money for the things you really want.** Owner-builders Betsy Hagerty and Tom McNamara built a beautiful house on a modest budget because they did plenty of up-front planning. Betsy wanted a suite of stainless kitchen appliances, including a high-end, ultra-quiet dishwasher, and reserved money for them from square one.

- **Do the footwork, then order online.** Betsy spent lots of time looking at materials in retail outlets. After they chose a manufacturer, Betsy and Tom located the items online, and usually saved money by buying direct from a manufacturer or distributor. Understandably, bricks-and-mortar retailers hate this strategy, but if you're willing to spend the time, you can make your material allowances go much, much further.

- **Persevere in your quest for just the right material.** Vermont owner builder Lizabeth Moniz haunted the showrooms that had materials she coveted, and made friends with the salespeople. When she saw a distinctive glass block window in a plumbing supply showroom, she knew it would be perfect for the shower enclosure in one of her bathrooms. It was a very expensive window, but she kept going back to look. Finally, the salesman told her that the display was coming down and she could have the window for $50 if she could take it away herself. She showed up with her pickup truck and a reciprocal saw and carried off her bargain!

Don't Scrimp Here!

Although there are many ways to save money outlined in this section, there are some parts of your home where a bargain may cost you in the long run.

It's tempting to cut corners on the big-ticket items, but don't do it. Here are traps you should avoid:

- Pay attention to warranties for expensive items such as roofing and siding. These are key elements to keep weather out of your home. If they do not carry warranties for a longer period than you plan to live in your home, you'll be replacing them down the road, which could be very expensive.

■ Don't choose the least expensive windows and doors in the style you like, just because they're cheap. It's true that openings—windows and doors—eat up a hefty percentage of the budget. But durability and energy efficiency count. Cheap windows might lower the budget when you build, but cost you thousands over many seasons of heating and cooling, not to mention the cost of replacement if they fail.

■ Don't think you can pay for your budget overruns by cutting significant elements out of your planned landscape. A home with a bare-bones yard looks raw and unfinished. Save money for this important component of "curb appeal."

Choose Your Features with Care

Everyone who builds a custom home wants features that will distinguish it from the standard model. Even if your budget is strictly domestic wine rather than champagne, you'll want to include a few special details. Make sure they're choices you'll always be glad you made:

■ Don't get talked into the latest, greatest feature just because "everyone has it." If you'll never use the $3,000 whirlpool tub with the $1,500 fittings, don't install it. Guard your budget for the things that are most important to you and your family.

■ Carefully consider the use of high-cost material that is also high-maintenance. For example, many stone products used for floors and countertops are not only expensive to buy and install, but they also require regular sealing and other upkeep. If you're not willing to ante up for regular care of your high-priced finishes, opt for lower-maintenance alternatives.

■ What's hot today may be oh-so-cold tomorrow. Remember huge, single-pane picture windows? Harvest gold and avocado green appliances? Boldly patterned and brightly colored wallpaper? What looks new and *now* will eventually be old, so try to stick with classic styles and finishes that can be updated with new furnishings or accessories.

Quality Control

Do you understand the differences between the grades of dimensional lumber? Plumbing pipe? Know which types of fasteners are suitable for exterior/damp location framing and finishing? If you don't, and you're contracting your own custom home, you must learn about how to judge materials and their suitability for a particular job.

As an owner-builder, such material specs should be in your contract, because you're paying for a level of quality in materials as well as labor. Understanding what terms such as "construction grade" or "#2 or better" lumber mean protects you from an unscrupulous sub or supplier, who might try to enhance his bottom-line by using lesser-grade materials.

Substandard materials can result in failed inspections, or a house that won't stand the test of time. In Appendix B, you'll find a list of online articles to help you make sense of the standards for building materials.

Green Building Products

A couple of years ago, you'd have to hunt for products that provide green benefits such as healthier air quality, or those made from recycled or renewable resources. It was also more difficult to find materials and equipment designed for increased energy efficiency.

That situation has changed radically; today's big-box building materials suppliers, and many equipment makers, have a wide range of products that will make it easier to be green.

See Appendix B for information sources for green products.

Specialized Materials

People generally like to include features that appeal to them personally, or are somehow unique, in their houses.

Often, this means searching out such details as vintage hardware or lighting fixtures, reclaimed wood floors, Victorian bathtubs or sinks, handmade stained-glass windows, or salvaged architectural elements from vintage houses.

Obviously, these are not materials that can be found instantly, even with the worldwide shopping reach of the Internet.

If you want to find this kind of material, you'll have to start your research early. See Appendix C for some great house parts resources.

Preventing Theft

When building begins, so will the deliveries of materials and equipment to the building site. And after materials are onsite, *they need to be safeguarded.*

As the general contractor, you will need to check in and record the materials received and stored onsite, or designate one person to do this important job. At very busy times when many people are working at once, you also need to be sure that materials stay where they are stored until they're used. Construction theft is a $1 billion-plus problem in the United States, and a larger one worldwide.

Of course, an experienced contractor has a protocol for preventing theft. Contractor Bill Lardi has been building houses for two decades. His wife, Amy Traversa, manages the company books and advises that just-in-time (JIT) delivery and a relationship with a good lumberyard are the key elements of their basic security strategy. One of the added values of a good contractor is that you also "hire" his relationship with his subcontractors and suppliers. Bill has been buying his materials through two supply firms for almost 20 years, and they jump to get him what he needs rather than risk losing his future business.

If you can't get JIT delivery, perhaps a rented trailer or truck that can be locked, or another secured storage location can discourage materials from walking offsite. However, Bill often hears of materials and tools disappearing from inside locked and unoccupied houses under construction. Bill offers a reminder: "Most contractors carry insurance against such theft. The cost of the insurance is built into a contractor's price as one of the overhead items that many do-it-yourselfers don't consider." Your insurance policy should offer protection against building site theft.

Another experienced builder, Steve Sferra, invested in a system made by DeWalt, a maker of construction-grade tools, which sends an alarm via cell-phone or e-mail if a site is disturbed. Although sites in developed neighborhoods are less vulnerable—neighbors pay attention to strange people and trucks—lightly populated, rural locations are often easy targets for thieves.

Materials Worksheets

Use the worksheets on the following pages to select, quantify, and price all the elements of your plans. As a guide, use the sample materials list developed by architect Rick Thompson and reproduced in Appendix C, or work from the 16-division checklist at the beginning of this section. Indicate whether the item is in stock or whether an order requires lead time; write down the lead time so you can include ordering it in your schedule.

Materials Worksheet

Item Name/Model Number	Manufacturer	Finish

Quantity	Price/Unit	In Stock/Lead Time	Source

Materials Worksheet

Item Name/Model Number	Manufacturer	Finish

	Quantity	Price/Unit	In Stock/Lead Time	Source

Materials Worksheet

Item Name/Model Number	Manufacturer	Finish

	Quantity	Price/Unit	In Stock/Lead Time	Source

Notes

Subcontractors 5

Building a house takes skill, brains, and muscle. As the general contractor, you'll be hiring all three. This section offers pointers to help you find and hire the best for your project.

Your Team

Here's an alphabetical listing of the professionals you'll encounter on the way to your certificate of occupancy. Of course, you'll hire some of these, such as the attorney or your architect, long before the actual building begins:

- Appraiser
- Asphalt/paving contractor
- Attorney
- Audiovisual equipment installer
- Bank loan officer
- Board of Health inspector (for the septic system)
- Building materials suppliers (multiple)
- Cabinet installer
- Carpet/linoleum contractor
- Central vacuum system installer
- Cleaning contractor
- Drywall installer/finisher
- Electrician
- Engineer (for certifying plans not completed and stamped by a licensed architect)
- Excavator
- Exterminator (if foundation must be treated)

- Fencing contractor, or mason for brick or stone walls
- Finish carpenter
- Footings contractor
- Foundation contractor
- Framer (carpenter)
- Gutter and downspout contractor
- Hardwood floor installer/finisher
- Home designer or architect
- HVAC contractor
- ICF (insulating concrete forms) contractor
- Independent home inspector
- Insurance agent
- Landscape architect
- Landscape contractor
- Licensed surveyor
- Local building inspector/code enforcement officer

- Mason
- Members of the local historical or zoning board
- Members of the local planning board
- Painter
- Plumber
- Portable toilet contractor
- Real estate agent
- Roofer
- Security system installer

- Septic system installer (if no municipal waste system)
- Siding contractor
- Testing services (when required, for soils, water, concrete)
- Tiling contractor
- Trash hauler
- Utility company representative(s)
- Waterproofing contractor
- Well driller (if no municipal water)

Of course, you'll find some subcontractors who can fill multiple jobs. But there's a great deal of work to be done, and as GC you'll hire and organize those who will make your plans a reality.

Pro Know-How

If you want specialized help for your interior design, kitchen, or landscape, or need advice on green building products and methods, don't wait until building is already in progress. Says Mac Rood, an architect and owner-builder himself, "Hire a landscape architect before the hole is dug, and the interior and kitchen designers, as well as any green building specialist, before the plans are complete. Don't bring them in late. Contractors and subcontractors are sure to hit you with change orders when the consultants decide to move a wall or change specs that the trades have already bid on and contracted for."

The Market for Subcontractors

First, a reality check. Because you are probably not a GC by trade, work on your project does not imply future work for the sub. You will be competing for subs with all the big builders and contractors in your area. In a hot market, this means that the best subs are in demand by their best sources of repeat work. In a slow housing market, the labor force will be hungrier and more accommodating.

Whether there's a housing boom or a bust, however, you can find good subs. Just allow more time in your schedule in seasons and markets when the construction trades are busy. You may have to wait for certain subcontractors, which will mean delaying those that come after.

Says architect Mac Rood, who teaches owner-builders how to handle their projects, "The less time you've been in business, the more time you should allow in your schedule." It's good advice. Even the best, most experienced builders sometimes have to wait for a particularly skilled sub whose services are essential to their project.

The Habits of Highly Effective Subcontractors

Here are some attributes to look for in any sub you hire:

- Phone calls are always returned. Starting with your inquiry, if grass grows beneath your feet before a prospect calls you back, it's not a good sign for the future.

- Good manners are essential. Not all subs are talkative people, but the good ones are always polite.

- Experience with a job such as yours (similar in size and scope) really does count. The sub may have installed beautiful kitchens, baths, or a great wraparound porch for your next-door neighbor. But if he's never worked on a brand-new house, the large job may exceed his grasp.

- A good sub will study your plans and specs and ask questions before he or she submits an estimate or bid. Subs don't like to waste their time: they want the most complete information on which to base their estimates.

- Verifiable references (names, phone numbers, addresses), of work recently done are good insurance. Ask for two of the three to be references that you can physically check out.

- A good sub is a team player. He can get along with the other subs, and takes his own responsibility seriously.

- Any good sub has the appropriate license, as well as workman's compensation insurance. Always ask for these as part of your interview. If the sub doesn't have them on his person, insist that he submit copies with his proposal.

Locating Good Subcontractors

Finding good professionals and tradespeople should not be too much of a problem:

- Start gathering information and references early. You don't need to be in hiring mode to talk with subcontractors. Your job still may be in the planning stage, but if you have a general idea of when you'll begin, you can prescreen the available workforce to find people who "click" with you and your project.

- If you own a house already, subcontractors who have done a good job with its repairs and improvements are a logical place to begin. Chances are they've worked on new construction, and they will probably know other subs you can interview.

- Subcontractors are always meeting other subcontractors. Drywall hangers know framing carpenters. Painters know finish carpenters. Plumbers know electricians.

When you find a sub you like, ask him for names of those with whom he likes to work.

■ Although they may not want to make recommendations, the local building inspector and local suppliers are aware of who's busy and who's paying their bills on time—both qualities that bode well. Let these sources know you're interested in finding good subs and would appreciate knowing who might be interested in bidding on a new job.

Hiring Subs

If you start finding subs long before you're ready to get started building, you'll have a good idea of who might be right, and also available, to work on your project.

What the Subs Need from You

First, a sub needs a general idea of when his or her services will be needed.

Second, because there is no structure to look at, your plans are the tradeperson's guide for the project. Every trade, from the excavator to the finish carpenter, will need to see your plans and specs to create an accurate estimate and/or bid.

To get bids that are realistic and comparable, you must know what you want.

If you are soliciting bids from multiple subs, you will need to provide each one with the same information. You can't ask one electrical contractor to bid on installing 30 recessed ceiling fixtures and the next one to bid on 45 if you want the bids to be comparable

After you've chosen your sub and contracted the work, changes in its scope will change the finances. Remember, after you break ground, change is costly.

To get realistic estimates from subcontractors:

■ Your plans should be as complete as you can make them.

■ You should know which materials you want to use.

■ You should clearly communicate the same information to any sub who is bidding against another for the same job.

Questions for the Subs

How many years have you been in business?

Can you tell me about the jobs you've worked on recently?

Who are some of the builders you work with?

Do you guarantee your work? For how long? (What you want to know here is that a sub will come back and fix anything that breaks within a given time period; the first year you're in the house is a reasonable window.)

What do you like about my plans? Is there anything about them that you question or would do differently? Why?

What are your payment requirements? (Tradespeople have different terms; not everyone is "net 30 days.")

May I see your workman's compensation insurance certificate and your local license? (Note that not every municipality or state has licensing requirements. You can ask the building department about this before you start interviewing.)

Questions for a Sub's References

Was this subcontractor easy to work with?

Did he work well with your architect (if he or she used one)?

Were you happy with the quality of his work?

Did he take responsibility for his work?

Did he show up on schedule? Finish on schedule?

Did his final cost match his bid? If not, why not?

Was he organized? Did he clean up after himself/workers at the end of each day? (If the sub doesn't clean after himself, you'll be pushing that broom!)

Were there any problems? If so, were you satisfied with how they were resolved? (Sometimes, people will hesitate to bring this up, unless *you* ask directly.)

Gathering Information

Make as many copies of the following form as you need. Store completed information sheets in this organizer until you file them.

Subcontractor Information

Subcontractor Information for (Job): _____

Name _____

Business name _____

Business address _____

_____

Phone _____ Fax _____

E-mail _____

Work skills (list all subcontracting skills that apply to this job)

_____

_____

_____

_____

_____

_____

_____

_____

Years in business _____

License number _____

Workman's Comp. Certificate _____

References (Customers)

Get at least three names and phone numbers of house projects done in the past two or three years.

Name _____   Phone _____

Date project completed _____

Notes on reference check

_____

_____

_____

_____

Name _____   Phone _____

Date project completed _____

Notes on reference check

_____

_____

_____

_____

Name _____   Phone _____

Date project completed _____

Notes on reference check

_____

_____

_____

_____

Keep in Mind

A house requires huge amounts of time and money to complete. Would you trust your life savings to an "investment manager" who arrived on your doorstep without references? Talk to your subs' previous customers and see how they worked with them. Ask the questions listed earlier. You don't want to be the unsuspecting customer who never bothered with the reference check and wound up with failed inspections or unfinished work.

Assembling Your Team

If you can find a good local carpentry team, often they will be instrumental in helping you find other subcontractors. A crew of three to five is good for an average-sized house, with a larger crew necessary for bigger projects.

An experienced excavator is also critical. He will be doing the earth moving, and in many cases will do your foundation work. Because accurate excavation and foundation work is critical to your project, an established contractor will have his own equipment (expensive), a crew who works regularly for him, and plenty of references.

Your building inspector, if he's willing to talk, can tell you about excavators in your area. Even if he won't give a recommendation, you might ask him if he's failed any foundations by anyone you're interviewing. That would be an excavating contractor you want to avoid.

Going to Bid

To keep your budget in check, you may want to bid out the expensive portions of your job, giving the subcontracts to the best bids among three or four bidders.

If your architect is handling this process for you, he can send out bidding packages, answer subs' questions, and receive the bids. However, if you're doing this task yourself, you'll have to allow time in the schedule.

Because there's nothing to look at but your construction documents, you will have to give each bidder a copy, complete with any specifications pertinent to their job, and be willing to answer any questions. To keep the process fair, you'll have to inform all bidders of additional information when you answer a question from one. (Fortunately, in this age of e-mail, this is less cumbersome than it used to be.)

Subs for the mechanicals in your house—HVAC, plumbing, electrical, and specialized equipment—will all need to have the same plans to work from, so if you're using stock plans without this information, you'll need to have these plans drawn by an architectural engineering or drafting firm, or meet with every sub and have them draw the same information on their floor plans.

When you ask for formal bids, everyone needs to submit their bid at the same time, and you need to give them all the same date when you will announce your decision (they like quick decisions).

In a hot housing market, it's tough to get the really good subs to bid; they've already got plenty of work. But if your housing market is slow, it may save you money to take the bidding route. Hungry contractors will keep their prices lean!

Develop Your Contact List

As you hire subcontractors for your project, you can list them in the front of this organizer. Check them off at the front of the Contact Lists section, then list further information in the address book–like spaces in the same section. Don't forget things such as ...

- Best time to reach them
- Name of the person who answers the phone (if there's an office)
- E-mail address

Keep the information sheets you gathered on the subs you met. You hope your final picks will stick, but if one doesn't pan out, you'll need to find a substitute—perhaps very quickly.

Getting the Best from Your Subs

As the general contractor, you'll be seeing quite a bit of the professionals and tradespeople you hire. Here are some suggestions on keeping the relationship positive and productive.

Pro Know-How

Says architect and owner-builder Mac Rood, "As GC, you'll be pulling the permits, calling the inspector, and managing the money. You'll sometimes be the broom pusher, when it's needed. And you will be the person to smooth the way between subs. As GC, you must be respectful of subs—ask framers to do what plumbers need. Always anticipate what's coming and prepare for it. Realistically, one of the criteria that the sub will use in deciding to work for you is whether he or she thinks you're up to the job. If you're not able to put in the time, it's a wise owner who hires someone—a retired contractor or carpenter, for example—who knows the trades and can act like a building superintendent on your behalf when decisions need to be made."

Tom McNamara, an owner-builder whose project went on for somewhat longer than anticipated because of site limitations, has five points for working with your subs:

- It's good to put yourself in a sub's shoes once in a while. Some of the jobs you're hiring them to do are very, very difficult, some are dirty, some are just downright uncomfortable. There is also the danger factor. Appreciate that for the most part, these people will work hard to build you a house within your budget.

- Most subs are not politicians, nor do they have great bedside manners. You need to make up for some of the skills they lack. Smile and be happy with what they are doing when they are doing it well.

- If you are unhappy with something, talk to the right person. The drywall hanger doesn't care if the plumber forgot to cap a pipe.

- If you change your mind even a little, it's going to cost *you* money. Be careful what you ask for.

- Be calm. That way if something does go wrong and you need to make an impact, you can.

Notes

You'll probably be jotting down names of contractors, phone numbers, and tips from lots of sources. Put those notes here until you get in touch with them.

_____

_____

_____

_____

_____

_____

_____

_____

_____

_____

_____

_____

_____

_____

_____

_____

_____

_____

_____

_____

_____

_____

_____

_____

_____

_____

_____

Suppliers

6

As the general contractor, you will do most of the materials purchasing, except when your sub's contacts and experience make his markup on materials worth the extra cost. This will be true in such areas as foundation pouring or rock blasting, unless you're a concrete or dynamite specialist! Finding reliable suppliers with quality inventory and can-do attitudes is an important part of your job. Here's how to do it.

Getting the Best Price/Quality/Value

Finding suppliers who are dependable, offer competitive prices, and stock quality materials may be as easy as a recommendation from someone you trust. Keep the following points in mind:

- **Know that biggest is not always best.** Most professional contractors find one or two local suppliers who provide reliable delivery and good payment terms. A local big-box home improvement store may not be able to provide the personalized service, so interview supplier prospects, just as you would your subcontractors.

- **Ask subs to recommend suppliers.** Subcontracting is a time-sensitive business, so these tradespeople need on-time delivery. They also need good payment terms: a little flexibility on payment due while they wait for contractors to pay them and discounts for quick payment. These are points that should interest you as well.

- **Look for the supplier with the best products available for the price.** A lumber delivery with two-by-fours that are twisted and cupped will anger you and frustrate your subs. If you ask for a certain grade, you want to be sure it will be delivered, and be able to return rejects. A reputation for quality is important.

Getting a General Contractor's Price

Because you're building a house, you'll be purchasing far more material than the average retail customer. It's okay to ask for a discount. Owner-builder Cynde Clark asked her framing/carpentry contractor to split the discount he received on materials. This saved her more money than the supplier offered her as an owner-builder-GC. Because she was only building a single house, the discount was not as deep as it was for the contractor, who used the supplier repeatedly. Her carpenter agreed. This worked for a few reasons:

- She knew costs in advance: the regular retail price, the price with her discount, and the price her sub was offered.
- She had a great relationship with the contractor.
- She took responsibility for checking out all the materials as they arrived.
- She was decisive and did not cause the contractor any problems with his supplier.

Good relationships with your main subs are always most important. If you get along and take the responsibility to supervise deliveries and pay as promised, you might be able to get better prices with suppliers.

Ready for Take-Off?

If you have a complete list of materials (such as the one at the end of this section), you can easily create a *take-off,* which is the complete list of materials needed for constructing your project, quantified for pricing and purchase.

A precise take-off is only possible if you have specs for the job that include the following:

- Quantity, types, sizes, and grades for all building materials
- Manufacturer, model, style number, quantity, and all pertinent information for any equipment that will be incorporated in construction

Any materials that have not been specifically selected must be accounted for by an *allowance*—an estimate of what it will cost to provide that material. If you were contracting with a GC and couldn't decide about an item, you would indicate this cost with a number signifying the amount you would allow for that piece of the job.

If your construction budget has too many allowances, you may be caught short of money late in the schedule when things come in at costs higher than anticipated. Although people try to shop smart, it's not always possible, and those ordering deadlines will creep up on you when you're building. Try not to have too many allowed-for items; they might be painful later on.

Preparing a Take-Off

Are you able to estimate the number of 2-by-4s, 6s, 10s, 12s, shingles, concrete, and so forth in your project? If an architect has not done this for you, and you've enlisted an architectural drafting/engineering firm to sign off on your plans, you may also want to ask them to prepare a materials take-off. Usually these companies have an estimator who works on staff or consults for them. They probably also have software that will provide a rough guide to materials costs—one that you'll want to firm up when you've made your supplier and subcontractor decisions.

Doing Your Own Take-Off

If you are familiar with estimating and have done materials lists for additions and renovations, you may want to create the materials take-off for your house. But unless construction estimating is part of your own business, it's a lot to take on. If you want to try, however, a good reference is Wayne DelPico's *Plan Reading & Material Takeoff* (see Appendix B).

Questions for Potential Suppliers

Depending on the area where you're building, you may have many supplier choices, or just a few. But to get the best materials, prices, and terms, you need to see how well each possible supplier can meet your requirements.

When you check out a supplier, bring your plans, specs, and materials lists with you. Be prepared for the questions they will ask you.

When you interview a supplier, ask to speak with a manager, and find out who handles accounts for contractors. Tell them you're general contracting your house, and looking for a supplier.

General Questions

Cover the basic information first. It's important to find out if a supplier's hours and policies will mesh with your needs. Ask:

- What are your hours of operation and delivery?
- How do I set up an account? (Get an application and a copy of one of their purchase orders.)
- Are there discounts for quick payment? A special discount for contractors? Finance charges after what date? (Often this is net 30 days after delivery, sometimes less.)
- How do I place an order? By phone? By fax? By e-mail? What is the procedure that they like you to follow? Is there a contact name and number for contractor orders?
- Are there delivery charges?
- What is your return policy?

Keep in Mind

Unanticipated extra charges for deliveries, or a percentage of the cost of returned merchandise, often called a *restocking charge,* can play havoc with your budget. Make sure you understand what the delivery charges will be (if they're not included in suppliers' prices) and if there is a restocking fee for returns. There are always returns.

Questions Specific to Your Project

Your project may require materials of a special type or size that the supplier may not keep in stock. Or the supplier may be able to offer specialized services that help you. Find out now.

- Are staples such as lumber, drywall, fasteners, shingles, and other basics I will need in quantity always in stock? (If your subs run low, you'll need quick turnaround.)

- What is the turnaround time from order to delivery for all the categories of material? (Go through the list with the supplier's rep.)

- Are there any materials you do *not* provide, so I can find another source?

- Will you be willing to do a materials take-off and price quote based on my plans? (Even if you've got one prepared on your own, you'll want to see how close their estimate will come to yours. Most suppliers will be willing to do this to get your business.)

Keep in Mind

Make sure to do a line-by-line comparison of any materials take-offs you get from suppliers, and your own estimator (from your architect or architectural engineer's office). Estimators have been known to leave out whole categories of materials.

Supplier Information Forms

Use these forms when you visit suppliers. Fill them out completely so that you can easily access the information you need. When you decide on your suppliers, enter their names and information in the Contact Lists at the front of this organizer.

Company name _____

Address _____

Phone _____ Fax _____

E-mail _____

Contact _____

Direct phone/extension/e-mail _____

Hours of operation _____

Delivery hours _____

Delivery charges _____

Delivery contact (if other than above):

Name _____

Phone _____ E-mail _____

Restocking fees _____

Order protocol _____

_____

_____

_____

Payment terms _____

Discounts _____

Special order time requirements for delivery (please list all that apply):

_____

_____

_____

Check all that apply:

☐ Materials take-off   ☐ Charge application   ☐ Sample PO

Other notes: _____

_____

_____

_____

Company name _____

Address _____

Phone _____ Fax _____

E-mail _____

Contact _____

Direct phone/extension/e-mail _____

Hours of operation _____

Delivery hours _____

Delivery charges _____

Delivery contact (if other than above):

Name _____

Phone _____ E-mail _____

Restocking fees _____

Order protocol _____

_____

_____

_____

Payment terms _____

Discounts _____

Special order time requirements for delivery (please list all that apply):

_____

_____

_____

Check all that apply:

☐ Materials take-off   ☐ Charge application   ☐ Sample PO

Other notes: _____

_____

_____

_____

Company name _____

Address _____

Phone _____ Fax _____

E-mail _____

Contact _____

Direct phone/extension/e-mail _____

Hours of operation _____

Delivery hours _____

Delivery charges _____

Delivery contact (if other than above):

Name _____

Phone _____ E-mail _____

Restocking fees _____

Order protocol _____

_____

_____

_____

Payment terms _____

Discounts _____

Special order time requirements for delivery (please list all that apply):

_____

_____

_____

Check all that apply:

☐ Materials take-off   ☐ Charge application   ☐ Sample PO

Other notes: _____

_____

_____

_____

Company name _____

Address _____

Phone _____ Fax _____

E-mail _____

Contact _____

Direct phone/extension/e-mail _____

Hours of operation _____

Delivery hours _____

Delivery charges _____

Delivery contact (if other than above):

Name _____

Phone _____ E-mail _____

Restocking fees _____

Order protocol _____

_____

_____

_____

Payment terms _____

Discounts _____

Special order time requirements for delivery (please list all that apply):

_____

_____

_____

Check all that apply:

☐ Materials take-off   ☐ Charge application   ☐ Sample PO

Other notes: _____

_____

_____

_____

Company name _____

Address _____

Phone _____ Fax _____

E-mail _____

Contact _____

Direct phone/extension/e-mail _____

Hours of operation _____

Delivery hours _____

Delivery charges _____

Delivery contact (if other than above):

Name _____

Phone _____ E-mail _____

Restocking fees _____

Order protocol _____

_____

_____

_____

Payment terms _____

Discounts _____

Special order time requirements for delivery (please list all that apply):

_____

_____

_____

Check all that apply:

☐ Materials take-off   ☐ Charge application   ☐ Sample PO

Other notes: _____

_____

_____

_____

Company name _____

Address _____

Phone _____ Fax _____

E-mail _____

Contact _____

Direct phone/extension/e-mail _____

Hours of operation _____

Delivery hours _____

Delivery charges _____

Delivery contact (if other than above):

Name _____

Phone _____ E-mail _____

Restocking fees _____

Order protocol _____

_____

_____

_____

Payment terms _____

Discounts _____

Special order time requirements for delivery (please list all that apply):

_____

_____

_____

Check all that apply:

☐ Materials take-off   ☐ Charge application   ☐ Sample PO

Other notes: _____

_____

_____

_____

Company name _____

Address _____

Phone _____ Fax _____

E-mail _____

Contact _____

Direct phone/extension/e-mail _____

Hours of operation _____

Delivery hours _____

Delivery charges _____

Delivery contact (if other than above):

Name _____

Phone _____ E-mail _____

Restocking fees _____

Order protocol _____

_____

_____

_____

Payment terms _____

Discounts _____

Special order time requirements for delivery (please list all that apply):

_____

_____

_____

Check all that apply:

☐ Materials take-off   ☐ Charge application   ☐ Sample PO

Other notes: _____

_____

_____

_____

Notes

Paperwork

7

A home-building project will produce a long paper trail. Keeping track of everything going on will require you to maintain meticulous files, and keep them up to date.

Having everything in writing—not only contracts, loan agreements, and purchase orders, but also meeting notes and e-mail exchanges—will save you from misunderstandings and lost time and money.

Your Master Filing System

Being able to put your hands on the right piece of paper at the crucial moment will serve you well. Consider arranging your papers around these five subjects:

- Money
- Plans and Materials
- Subcontractors
- Schedule
- Important/Legal Documents

Whether you use a file box, an accordion file, or a thick, D-ring notebook, organizing your papers this way will make finding important documents much easier. Create a system that works for you, and stick to it.

From the Home Team

"Stay organized. Time is money for everyone. No matter how small the detail, follow up everything you discuss in writing—by e-mail or with a fax. Work to be clear and concise."

—Siobhan Daggett-Terenzi, owner-builder

File Checklists

Each of these checklists has blank lines to fill in if you have other types of documents to include.

Money

- ☐ Project budget
- ☐ Loan application, supporting documents
- ☐ Loan agreement
- ☐ Draw (disbursement) schedule
- ☐ Requisitions for loan disbursements
- ☐ Purchase orders
- ☐ Invoices (payable)
- ☐ Invoices (paid)
- ☐ Change orders
- ☐ Lien waivers (You may want to attach copies of the signed lien waivers to paid subcontractor invoices. At the end of the project, these will be part of your legal document file.)
- ☐ _____
- ☐ _____
- ☐ _____

Plans and Materials

- ☐ Architect/owner-builder agreement
- ☐ Plans (all phases, from preliminary sketches to construction-ready drawings)
- ☐ Master construction document set
- ☐ Additional sets of construction documents
- ☐ Additional detail drawings
- ☐ Correspondence with designer/architect/engineer
- ☐ Meeting/conversation notes (re: plans)
- ☐ Building materials information: spec sheets, brochures, magazine articles
- ☐ Finish materials information: paint, wood, tile, chips, swatches, photos, samples, etc.
- ☐ Specifications
- ☐ Materials lists
- ☐ Materials take-off

☐ Warranties (materials and equipment)

☐ _____

☐ _____

☐ _____

Subcontractors

☐ Subcontractor bids by category

☐ Workman's compensation policies (photocopies)

☐ Accepted bids

☐ Subcontractor contracts

☐ _____

☐ _____

☐ _____

Schedule

☐ Preliminary schedule

☐ Master schedule

☐ _____

☐ _____

☐ _____

Important/Legal Documents

☐ Legal correspondence, notes, e-mails related to meetings and conversations

☐ Property title/deed

☐ Survey

☐ Real estate tax records

☐ Insurance documents (builder's risk/homeowner)

☐ Zoning variance (if required)

☐ Testing results (well, water, septic, etc.)

☐ Permits

☐ Inspection records and demands

☐ Certificate of Occupancy

☐ _____

☐ _____

☐ _____

Money Paperwork

Everything related to money—acquiring it and spending it—should go in this file. Here are some critical money documents.

Project Budget

This document will be in development throughout the project. No matter how precise a budget you create, there will always be something that comes higher than expected. Likewise, problems you anticipate may not materialize, lowering an entry here and there.

Although this book has places for estimated and actual costs (in every section of Part 2), you may want to generate a complete budget spreadsheet that you can continually update. Use this book as you supervise the ongoing project, and then update your numbers on a master spreadsheet.

Loan Application

In Section 1, you will find a list of materials you should gather for your application to the bank. Make photocopies of those documents you keep in a safe or deposit box and mark the copies with the location of the original.

Draw (Disbursement) Schedule

This is the schedule that enables you to draw funds from your construction loan. As you approach benchmarks, you'll need to prepare the appropriate form and schedule the bank's inspector.

Disbursement Requisition Form

Banks usually have their own document for you to use to request a draw. You don't want to have to hunt for one at a crucial juncture; keep a supply in your money file.

Purchase Orders

A lot of material and equipment gets delivered to your site. But sometimes the wrong materials get delivered, or you don't get the complete order, or something arrives damaged.

Use purchase orders to keep your accounts straight. If you set up accounts with your suppliers, you'll be able to track everything that comes and goes.

Most suppliers indicate the account name and the name of the person making the order on their purchase order. This enables you to know who placed an order, if it wasn't yourself.

Keep copies of these forms handy so that you can use them to fax in your orders when necessary.

Keep in Mind

It may require some fancy footwork on your part, but as GC you should be onsite for materials deliveries. It's the only way you can check and sign off on the order's correctness and condition. You'll need to stay in close touch with supplier dispatchers to time your presence for deliveries.

Invoices

Keep separate files to track paid and unpaid invoices. It's always a good practice to write the date and check number directly on the paid invoice, in case you have to track this information down later.

Change Orders

After your plans are set and your subcontractors are working, any substantive changes you make can be reflected in the costs of the project. The higher costs are recouped by the contractor (or returned to you, in the case of lower costs) by means of an agreement with the subcontractor, called a *change order*.

You can use a standard form (available from your architect or the local office of the American Institute of Architects—find your local office online at www.aia.org/components_map) or create your own. Change orders should be dated and numbered sequentially, so that corresponding plan changes or new detail drawings can be referenced to the changes.

Here's the information needed for a change order:

- Date
- Project name ([your name] house)
- Project address
- Change order number (number sequentially)
- Description of change to be made
- Contract parties in this change:
  - Owner
  - Subcontractor
  - Other (e.g., architect or designer)
- Drawing or detail number

- Original amount of contract
- Cost of proposed change (+ or –, indicate which)
- New contract amount
- Schedule change due to increase or decrease of work
- Signature and date from all contract parties in the change order agreement

If you draft your own change order form, you may want to run it by your attorney.

Keep a supply of these forms in your money file.

Lien Waivers

When a subcontractor has completed his or her contracted work on your project, and you have paid in full, you should receive a signed *lien waiver* from that subcontractor. Banks will often furnish copies of this document, as an unpaid contractor can encumber the clear title to property by placing a so-called mechanic's lien on that property. Such liens have derailed many a closing. Be sure to have your subcontractor sign (and notarize, if necessary) this form. If your subcontractor requires a cashier's check to sign off on the waiver, it's worth the few extra dollars the bank will charge.

Plans and Materials Paperwork

This material, which includes the construction drawings, will be referred to constantly during the building process. You'll want to keep the construction drawings in a portfolio case, or some other container, so that they can be protected from dirt and damage. There are other suggestions later in this section for keeping other construction-related documents secure.

Architect/Owner-Builder Agreement

See Section 3 regarding the parameters of architectural work on a residential project. You will need to draft a contract that covers all the work you expect from the architect.

For work outside the contract parameters, your agreement should stipulate a per hour or per diem fee and expense allowances.

As with any legal agreement, have your attorney review the agreement before you sign it.

Drawings (Schematic Through Construction)

As you receive each new set of drawings, from the conceptual to the final set of construction documents, be sure to date each group.

You will probably want to make a separate folder, slot, or binder section for each set of drawings. Sometimes going back to an old set will help you solve a problem that emerges later.

Construction Drawings: The Master Set

Whenever a change is made, a drawing added, or a new requirement attached to your project, the master set of plans should be changed and initialed by you and the architect. From this set, you can work with subs to revise their work accordingly.

Usually, the architect will make a notation referring to a change order or other document that alters the plans. This kind of detail is necessary to accurately track the project as it evolves from the original construction documents.

Additional Detail Drawings

When a change will structurally alter the plans, additional drawings to illustrate the change may be needed, for the subs as well as the building department. Keep these on file, dated and approved where necessary.

Correspondence and Meeting Notes Regarding Plans and Drawings

Keep written communications in chronological order. Circulate copies of meeting notes to all involved, so that they can be immediately modified if need be. If you communicate with the architect and subs by e-mail, keep hard copies of the e-mails in this file.

Be sure to keep everyone in the loop. Copy your subs when you communicate with the architect, and your architect when communicating with the subs.

You may want to take notes in a spiral or composition notebook, so you can review previous meetings and make sure all the details have been followed up.

Try to have one meeting a week with the major players onsite: the architect, sub(s), and you, the owner-builder/GC. Use your notes to send minutes to the parties involved. Written documentation is essential when differences of opinion or memory arise.

Keep in Mind

Plug-in external hard drives are a good way to keep back-up documents. It only takes a couple of seconds to back up these files daily. Losing your written records can cause much confusion, not to mention legal and financial problems. It's worth a few dollars and a few minutes a day to prevent these headaches.

Material and Equipment Warranties

Many of the materials and most of the equipment you purchase for the house will come with some kind of warranty. Keep the warranties in a folder (or folders) in the Plans and Materials section of your file.

Material and equipment warranties are usually accompanied by installation and use and care instructions. To keep the warranty in force, make sure the material or equipment is installed "according to manufacturers' instructions." Indicate this element in all written contracts with subs, in case something goes wrong after installation. Then the argument is between sub and manufacturer.

Many appliances, materials, and pieces of equipment are warranted for long periods. To keep track of the warranty period, *note the date that the warranted material is placed in use. Write this date directly on the warranty.* That date is the beginning of the warranty period.

Subcontractor Files

These are all your legal agreements with your subcontractors. Keep them secured and filed for easy reference.

Workman's Comp/License Information

You should be sure that the sub's license and workman's compensation policy are in force. Get copies of both from contractors you're using, and keep them on file.

Accepted Bids

In addition to accepted bids, keep information on your second and third choices, in case a relationship with a chosen sub goes sour or doesn't work out for some reason. File these under "Alternative Subs."

Contracts

You will want contracts with your subs. Whether you use pre-written forms that you customize, or write your own (with your attorney's advice), each one should contain certain components.

Contract Party Information

The names, titles, addresses, and phone numbers of all parties should be on the contract. A boilerplate contract will identify each party with language such as "Hereafter referred to as _____" to provide a title for each party in the contract (e.g., "owner," "sub-contractor," "builder," and so on).

Project Scope

"Dig a foundation" is not a sufficient description for your contract with the excavator. When describing the scope of work for your subcontractor, be as specific as possible about the full extent of the task to be performed, the materials to be used, and the performance of the finished installation. If you want equipment of certain sizes and efficiencies, and the sub will be purchasing it, you must specify what you want. You can attach copies of the specifications from your construction documents, and refer to them in the contract.

Project Cost

Indicate the total amount of payment, as well as the disbursement schedule, indicating any completion benchmarks required for the disbursements. If you are providing a down payment on the work, indicate this in the contract.

Allowances

If there are elements of the job for which the sub is responsible but you have not yet determined the specifics, you must include a specific allowance in the contract, or indicate that you will provide the material.

Schedule

Your contract should include start and finish dates for the contracted work, though these dates may be hard to enforce because of unanticipated problems. And it's hard to prove that any delay is solely the responsibility of the sub.

However, you can build a carrot-and-stick approach into your contract if time is really of the essence. You can include a clause that levies a per-diem charge for real losses you incur (rent you're paying to live elsewhere, travel expenses, and so on) if the sub is late with his finish. Most subs will not be happy with such a clause, so if you put a "stick" in the contract, you might also consider a "carrot": a cash bonus for every day the contractor finishes ahead of schedule. Do indicate, however, that all work must be of workmanlike quality and meet local code and inspection requirements. Make it clear that a quick-and-dirty job does not earn an incentive.

In Case of Change Orders

Include in your contract the procedure for handling change orders and how work outside the contract's scope will be billed. Is the arrangement for time and materials? If so, how much per hour, per person? If the sub will purchase additional materials or rent additional equipment, will he charge a percentage above the invoice as a contractor's surcharge for profit and overhead?

Insurance/License

Your sub should state in the contract that he carries insurance, and if required, is licensed to do the stipulated work in your jurisdiction.

Warranty

Most good contractors will guarantee their own labor for one year from its completion. Put this language in the contract.

Problems between owner-builders/general contractors and their subs often crop up in the execution of this warranty clause. For example, shingles that blow off a roof are a common warranty problem with new houses. The manufacturer may say that the roofer installed them improperly; the roofer may say that the product did not perform as warranted.

If you have the manufacturer's warranty, the stated warranty in your contract with your sub, and specific contract language requiring that the sub perform the installation in accordance with manufacturer's requirements, the two of *them* will have to fight over the repair and hopefully leave you out of it.

Contingencies

How does a contract allow for unforeseen circumstances? This often occurs in the excavation and site work phases, when unexpected problems are unearthed by earth-moving equipment.

Rather than include a cost factor for potential problems, such as ledge rock or big boulders, you can stipulate that in case of such problems, they will be dealt with by a formula—figuring the unit cost (per cubic yard in the case of rock, for example) for excavation and removal. If there is additional equipment required, note the unit cost (per hourly rental, for example) of such equipment.

Resolving Disputes

Contract disputes can get ugly. In case payment problems involving incomplete or unsatisfactory work arise, you may want to insert language in each contract that submits such disputes to independent arbitration.

Consult your attorney or the American Arbitration Association (www.adr.org) for more information.

Schedule File

Your schedule will evolve as you acquire more information and make final decisions about budget, plans, materials, subs, and suppliers. Even as construction begins, the schedule is a fluid document, changing with the weather and unexpected glitches.

See Section 8 for setting up your schedule; it provides a sample and then worksheets for you to fill in.

Although it's convenient to carry your schedule in this organizer, it's probably good to have the scheduling information on a computer spreadsheet (don't forget to back this up every time you add or subtract a notation).

As the schedule evolves, make a chronological file of the schedule revisions. Date each one so you're always looking at the most up-to-date document.

Important/Legal Documents File

It's okay to keep copies of files in your trunk or backseat, but the original documents (except for permits, which must be posted onsite) belong in your home safe or safety deposit box. Keep copies in your carry-around file containers, with the location of the original indicated on the copy. From time to time, you may need to produce original documents, so you have to be able to locate them quickly.

Notes

Schedule

8

As you develop budget numbers, talk to banks, refine your plans, start making decisions about materials and equipment, and interview potential subcontractors, you probably have construction start and finish dates in mind. Figuring out whether this imaginary timeline can synchronize with the house you're planning takes some work.

At the beginning of any project, everyone feels enthusiastic and optimistic. After the work starts, the realities of weather delays, subcontractor delays, delivery backorders, inspection delays, re-inspection requirements (uh-oh!), draw schedule delays, and innumerable other small glitches will dampen that optimism a bit.

Build in More Time Than You Think You'll Need

Although an experienced contractor is familiar with the juggling required to get a house completed, you are not. As architect, design-builder, and owner-builder Mac Rood acknowledges, "The less experience you have, the more time you should build into your schedule."

Many people will tell you that you can build a house in six months. A fairly detailed 2,500-plus-square-foot custom house can be done on such a schedule, but think longer—nine months to a year is common, particularly if you have more square footage, intricate detailing and finishes, or other complexities.

Owner-builder Siobhan Daggett-Terenzi started her home in late April and moved in six months later. Hers was the quickest finish among the owner-builders interviewed; most took about twice as long.

Keep in Mind

Put a little flex in your schedule, even if you are completely confident your project will come in on time. Banks generally put time limits on construction loans, and you should try to secure a loan that gives you more time than you think you'll need. Better to finish early than to have to beg the bank for more time and scramble to secure a bridge loan.

Create Your Schedule

For the details of each general category of work, refer to Part 2. This will give you an idea of the scope of work, the number of subcontractors involved, and the difficulty of getting the work done under unfavorable conditions. Obviously, after the house is closed in, interior work is not susceptible to weather delays.

Schedule Details

Many of the tasks listed in this section occur at more than one point in the schedule. For example, plumbers come in at several junctures:

- If you're building on a slab, they run and install pipe beneath the slab before it's poured.
- They rough-in pipes before the walls are insulated and closed in with drywall.
- In the finish phase, they install the fixtures and fittings at every water location.

The "Averages"

Every residential construction project is unique: subject to local laws and inspection protocols and having its own site, plan, materials, and labor. The best way to work out your schedule is to find out the timeline for all the materials and labor for your project.

Many "contract your own house" authors will give you an ambitious timeline and insist that it's possible for you to cram all the details you want into your house, and do it in six months. The reality is somewhat different. Many of these authors are professional builders and contractors whose contacts and experience help them move quickly. Although good planning and organization will keep your project moving, be realistic about your own project.

Timely Deliveries

Doors and windows require an order and deposit early in the sequence, well in advance of delivery and installation. This order is critical because a delay in window and door installation will prevent all the rough-in work from happening.

Equipment, fixtures, fittings, and materials for the finish portions of your house—such things as imported tile and stone, custom cabinetry, and special order moldings—need to arrive with the subs who will install them. If your material has not arrived, your subs can't work, thus changing your schedule and disrupting a smooth parade of workpeople.

Be sure to indicate order dates for long lead-time items on your schedule. Otherwise, you'll have unhappy subs and a schedule that goes off the rails.

Schedule Must-Do: Bank and Building Department Inspections

Part 2 mentions a number of possible inspections required by the health and building departments. Additionally, your bank will most likely require inspections prior to issuing your draw checks. Make sure that you've indicated these requirements in your schedule.

In my town in New York, the building and health department inspection list is daunting. Here's a list of their inspection requirements:

- Footings inspection; forms and soil
- Before backfill of foundations
- Waterproofing and exterior drains
- Before slab pour: gravel, vapor barrier, reinforcement
- Framing inspection
- Rough electrical
- Rough plumbing
- Rough HVAC
- Fireplace (three for masonry; three for modular fireplace)
- Insulation
- Drywall before taping
- Final plumbing test
- Smoke detector test
- Final building inspection
- Final electrical inspection
- Final health department inspection for septic
- Well driller's report

Your building department may not be so rigorous, but be sure to build its schedule, and the bank's, into your sequence. *Mark each point where an inspection will be required on your schedule.*

Inspectors are a serious bunch; if you forget the rough-in inspections, the inspector will not hesitate to tear out drywall and insulation to see the work. Neglecting to have and pass an inspection can be a serious and expensive mistake.

Schedule Format

Using your own timeline, fill in the weeks beginning with your proposed start date (when you have the building permit and the money and you're legally and financially ready to begin).

Then fill in the blocks next to each task for the length of time each task will take, going sequentially from left to right. For example, your plumbing contractor may be onsite to run pipe beneath your slab, then to rough-in the house system, then to do the finish work. Next to the "Plumbing" entry, you'll shade (or mark an X or put a line running through the box) three separate sets of blocks for these tasks in the correct date column to indicate when this work will happen in the schedule.

The timeline has four pages; feel free to photocopy these so you can work out all the details, marking the spots for inspection dates and materials orders in their proper place in the schedule.

Week #	1	2	3	4	5	6	7	8	9	10	11	12	13
Weeks 1–13													
Dates													
Work													
Site prep.													
Clearing													
Staking													
Excavation													
Foundation													
Slab													
Backfill													
Framing													
Windows													
Doors													
Chimney													
Roofing													
Siding													
Trim (Ext.)													
HVAC													
Plumbing													
Electrical													
Other Mechanicals:													
Insulation													
Drywall													
Hardwood													
Floor underlayment													
Tile													
Carpet													
Paint													
Trim (Int.)													
Garage													
Porch													
Landscape													
Driveway													
Cleaning													
Final ins.													

Weeks 14–26													
Week #	14	15	16	17	18	19	20	21	22	23	24	25	26
Dates													
Work													
Site prep.													
Clearing													
Staking													
Excavation													
Foundation													
Slab													
Backfill													
Framing													
Windows													
Doors													
Chimney													
Roofing													
Siding													
Trim (Ext.)													
HVAC													
Plumbing													
Electrical													
Other Mechanicals:													
Insulation													
Drywall													
Hardwood													
Floor underlayment													
Tile													
Carpet													
Paint													
Trim (Int.)													
Garage													
Porch													
Landscape													
Driveway													
Cleaning													
Final ins.													

Week #	27	28	29	30	31	32	33	34	35	36	37	38	39
Weeks 27–39													
Dates													
Work													
Site prep.													
Clearing													
Staking													
Excavation													
Foundation													
Slab													
Backfill													
Framing													
Windows													
Doors													
Chimney													
Roofing													
Siding													
Trim (Ext.)													
HVAC													
Plumbing													
Electrical													
Other Mechanicals:													
Insulation													
Drywall													
Hardwood													
Floor underlayment													
Tile													
Carpet													
Paint													
Trim (Int.)													
Garage													
Porch													
Landscape													
Driveway													
Cleaning													
Final ins.													

Weeks 40–52													
Week #	40	41	42	43	44	45	46	47	48	49	50	51	52
Dates													
Work													
Site prep.													
Clearing													
Staking													
Excavation													
Foundation													
Slab													
Backfill													
Framing													
Windows													
Doors													
Chimney													
Roofing													
Siding													
Trim (Ext.)													
HVAC													
Plumbing													
Electrical													
Other Mechanicals:													
Insulation													
Drywall													
Hardwood													
Floor underlayment													
Tile													
Carpet													
Paint													
Trim (Int.)													
Garage													
Porch													
Landscape													
Driveway													
Cleaning													
Final ins.													

Week #	53	54	55	56	57	58	59	60	61	62	63	64	65
Weeks 53–65													
Dates													
Work													
Site prep.													
Clearing													
Staking													
Excavation													
Foundation													
Slab													
Backfill													
Framing													
Windows													
Doors													
Chimney													
Roofing													
Siding													
Trim (Ext.)													
HVAC													
Plumbing													
Electrical													
Other Mechanicals:													
Insulation													
Drywall													
Hardwood													
Floor underlayment													
Tile													
Carpet													
Paint													
Trim (Int.)													
Garage													
Porch													
Landscape													
Driveway													
Cleaning													
Final ins.													

Notes

Part 2

Construction

Part 2 puts the steps of construction in sequence, from pre-building work to physical preparation of the site and the foundation. Then come the tasks that make your house start to look like a home: framing and sheathing the walls and roof, installing windows and doors, and applying siding. Sections 9 through 12 walk you through this relatively rapid segment of construction.

With Section 13 the process moves inside, and you begin to conduct a virtual orchestra of subcontractors and inspectors. Section 14 focuses on construction and completion of porches, decks, and garages. While the outside crew is shaping exterior details, the finish work, covered in Section 15, goes on inside. If your construction crew is an orchestra, then Section 16 is your musical score. This Master Tracker enables you to put every facet of your project on paper.

You'll make good use of the checklists provided in every section, as one by one, each task is completed.

It's time to put on your work boots and start the real physical and mental exercise of getting your house built!

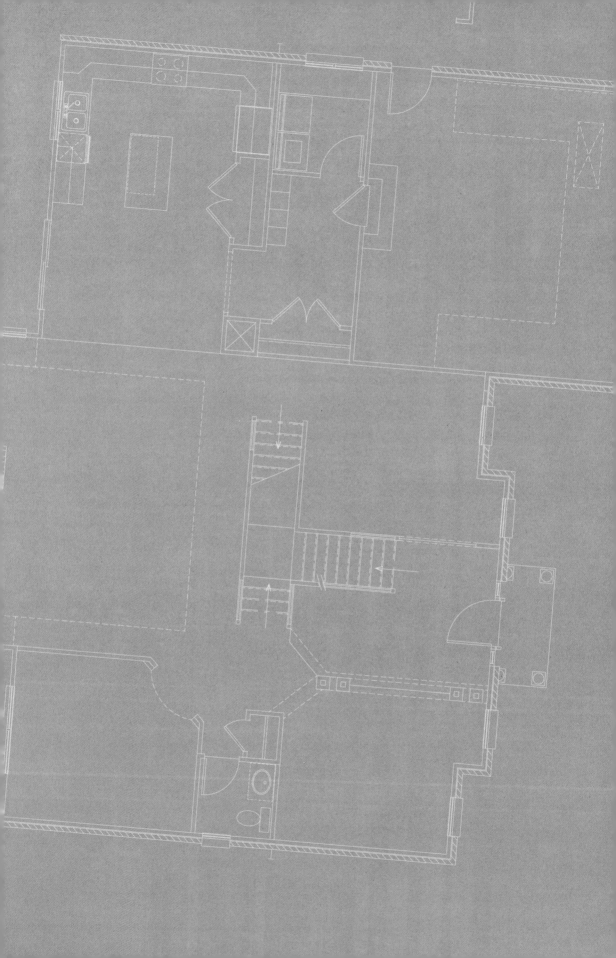

Pre-Building

9

Before your subs start building, you need to be sure that your plans are legal and meet all local zoning requirements. You must have the proper permits. You need to be prepared for the arrival of large quantities of equipment, material, and workers. You need to ready your finances to write substantial checks.

Begin with a checklist of the work that you will complete in this phase of construction.

For an expanded explanation of each task, read the overview pages of this section, which follow the list.

Pre-Building Checklist

Use this checklist as a quick guide to pre-building tasks. Refer to your Contact Lists for the appropriate names and numbers.

Work for This Phase	Contact
☐ Know the local building laws	Building inspector, local gov't. rep, attorney
☐ Cash on hand for pre-draw expenses	Your banker, or financial advisor
☐ Construction documents (review)	Building inspector
☐ Construction documents (revise)	Licensed design pro: engineer, architect
☐ Accessible deed for your lot, title insurance	Attorney, town clerk
☐ Driveway right-of-way	Inspector, Highway Dept.
☐ Builder's risk insurance policy	Insurance agent
☐ Permit for well	Inspector, Board of Health
☐ Permit for septic tank and field	Inspector, Board of Health
☐ Installation of well	Well driller
☐ Well water test	Certifying agency
☐ Installation septic	Septic installer
☐ Inspect septic tank and field	Inspector, Board of Health

Work for This Phase	Contact
☐ Submit survey, plans, and permit applications	Building Dept.
☐ Test hole at building site	Excavation sub
☐ Arrangements for site security	Suppliers
☐ Obtain any remaining approvals	Reps from planning and zoning, historical society, local design board, attorney
☐ Obtain necessary permits	Building inspector
☐ Arrange for sanitary facility and waste/carting service	Sanitary/carting services
☐ Order utility hookups	Utility rep
☐ Arrange for temporary electric	Electrical sub service
☐ Close construction loan	Bank, loan company, attorney

Pre-Building Overview

As the planning nears completion, a few important details remain before the backhoe and bulldozer arrive. You need to check that all is in order before the heavy lifting starts.

Every jurisdiction is a bit different. In some rural areas, there are fewer people looking over your shoulder as you build. In others, such as the established and rapidly growing suburb where I live, even if something gets by the building inspector, your neighbor may be all too eager to inform the authorities. Don't leave the door open for anything to disrupt the smooth flow of work.

Once the construction clock is ticking, you don't want the schedule interrupted by the building inspector, or some other municipal, legal, or financial roadblock. The next sections look at the details to take care of now.

Keep in Mind

If you are building in a quiet or densely populated neighborhood, the movement of construction equipment, workers, and materials may rattle your neighbors. Many people dislike disruption, and can wreak havoc if they start calling the building inspector or police because the noise, traffic, or general bedlam upsets them—even if everything you're doing is permitted by local laws. Introduce yourself to your neighbors; give them your cell phone or other direct phone number, so they call you *first* if something at the building site disturbs them. Let them know when construction will start. Head off potential problems before they begin.

Know Local Building Laws

Does the town where your site is located have ...

- Noise ordinances?
- Specific days and times when construction activity is not allowed?
- Conservation or environmental restrictions that could impact the way you clear or landscape your property?

Make sure you know the rules. Your building inspector, local government representative, or real estate attorney can familiarize you with relevant laws.

Disregarding local ordinances can mean fines or costly delays of your project. Pleading ignorance is not an option. Know the local regulations, and make sure you and your subs abide by them.

Have Cash on Hand for Pre-Draw Expenses

The money needs to start flowing before the bank issues checks. Make sure you're ready. If you intend to sell stocks or make other financial moves to raise this cash, do it before construction starts.

Review/Revise the Construction Documents

In bidding out your project and hiring your subcontractors, you may have made decisions that alter the plans you will submit to obtain your building permit. For example, you and your HVAC subcontractor may have decided to change the route of a duct run, or you decided to add recessed lighting where none were planned.

Remember: *The least expensive change to your project is a change to the plans, before building begins.*

Now is the time to finalize the changes:

- To be safe, run the changes by the building inspector; he'll be able to tell you if any of your changes could affect the legality or code-worthiness of your project.
- Adjust the drawings (have your licensed design professional indicate the changes on the plans, and initial them).
- Adjust the budget if there are additions or subtractions to labor and/or material costs.
- Clear the changes with the appropriate sub(s) and make sure that contract prices or estimates are changed before work begins. Adjust and initial contract changes.

File the Deed and Title Insurance

Put these papers where you can get to them quickly: in a safe deposit box or with your attorney. Have your lawyer review these documents, particularly if there are easements granted to you or your neighbors that affect your property.

Keep a copy of these items in your "important documents" file.

Secure Your Builder's Risk Insurance Policy

As GC you are liable for any accidents or other losses that occur on the building site. The bank that provides your loan will insist that you insure against these risks, so now is the time to obtain the policy. Contact your insurance agent.

Make Sure Your Proposed Driveway Is a Legal Right-of-Way

Depending on the road frontage that allows access to your property, you may need clearance from local, county, or state jurisdictions to make what is called a *curb cut,* or road access point for your driveway. Check with the building inspector; he or she can refer you to the appropriate highway department for paperwork or permits.

Friends of mine who should have known better (the husband is a builder) assumed that they could access their lot via a neighbor's driveway. Their project was stopped, and they spent several months in court and thousands of dollars to obtain road access. It was a miserable experience, tainting what should have been the happy culmination of years of dreaming and planning.

Obtain Well Permit, Install and Inspect (If Required)

If water does not flow to your home from a municipal or other public water system, now's the time to schedule your water well driller. If required, obtain a permit to drill the well. You must have an inspection after the well is dug.

Obtain Permit for Septic System, Install and Inspect (If Required)

If your lot is not serviced by a sewer system, you will also need to install a septic system. Now is the time to obtain the permit, usually from the county Board of Health. After the sub installs the septic tank and field, it will be inspected by the permitting agency.

Well Water Test (If Required)

This may also be part of the approval process for your well. If it is, have the water tested as required and keep the test results with your other important documents.

Submit Applications, Fees, and Supporting Documents for Building Permit

If all goes well, this *may* be your last hurdle with the building department before construction starts. Find out how long it will take for permits to be issued. The department will call you if anything is missing, which might be a trip or two on your part, to fill in blanks. If you've followed the instructions to the letter, your next step will be picking up the permits.

Excavate a Test Hole Near the Building Site (Optional)

If your home site turns out to have ledge rock, an underground stream, or another disturbance in the excavation area, this may compromise your site and mean greater expense. Rock equals blasting, and blasting is expensive. So some people excavate a test hole near the home site to look for such obstructions before digging starts.

If your lot is in an area where large rocks in the soil or shallow subterranean streams are not common, this is an unnecessary step. But if you're in a part of the country that was scraped by glaciers and is dotted with rock formations or has a high water table, it may be worth the expense. Excavation is costly, but blasting rock is costlier. And building over an underground stream is no way to keep a basement dry!

Arrange for Site Security

"Just in time" delivery comes in handy after building starts. You don't want to leave valuable building materials unguarded at the building site.

Owner-builder Patti Garbeck learned her lesson the hard way. She bought a large parcel on a remote dirt road in backcountry Vermont. Lumber for her house was stolen from the site before work began. "It was not the welcome to the neighborhood I was expecting," she recalls.

Don't let it happen to you. A few weeks will pass before the house can be closed in and locked. Building sites in upscale, well-developed neighborhoods are less vulnerable—the neighbors pay attention to unusual activity in these areas—but remote or urban lots are susceptible to theft and vandalism. It's a billion-dollar problem for professional builders.

Most large suppliers of building materials can refer you to products and service companies that can assist with site security. Locking rental sheds and pods, security fences, and video monitoring can protect construction sites.

Remember these points when considering security for your own building site:

- Work closely with the suppliers to take delivery of materials when they are needed, not before. You and the subs should be on the site when deliveries are made.

- Keep the materials area neat and organized. Stack and cover the lumber pile if materials remain at the end of the day.

- Check with local law enforcement about construction theft in your area. If it is a problem, beef up your security plan. Ask for advice from your subs, who may be more familiar with the security situation for your location.

Obtain Additional Required Approvals in Writing

If your property is in a neighborhood or district that gets scrutiny outside the building department, you've probably already submitted your plans to the local water commission, planning and zoning board, or historic district or design committee. Make sure that all these potential impediments to your project are comfortable with your plans. If you need certification from any of these bodies, get your written approvals *now*. File these forms or certificates with your other important documents.

Obtain Building Permit and Other Required Permits

Obtain your building permit and any other permits required by the bank providing your construction financing; you will post these documents when construction begins. Because the building permit is generally posted outside, be sure to have it laminated.

Arrange for Utility Hookup, Sanitary Facilities, and Waste Disposal

Contact your local utilities to get temporary water and electric service installed. You may need to fill out applications and pay fees for this step.

Also essential are sanitary facilities and large containers for construction waste. Workers will need a port-o-john onsite, as well as a place to discard building waste. Because of safety considerations, most municipalities will not allow builders to dump waste in a trench; containers must be hauled away as they are filled.

Let these service companies know that work is about to start.

Close on Your Construction Loan

At least a week before your scheduled closing, make sure that the bank has everything it needs to prepare all the closing documents. If you are unsure, call the loan officer for a closing checklist. Usually this is a part of the papers you received when your financing was approved.

Double-check everything; if you have any questions, consult the bank and your attorney.

Be sure you understand:

- All costs and fees due at closing
- Completion benchmarks for draws and the lender's inspection procedures

When your loan is closed, the real excitement—the construction phase—can begin.

Prepare to Be GC

You're at the start of a process that will put your management and organizing skills to the test. Here are some pointers from owner-builder Tom McNamara:

- **Be there.** Onsite. Every day, or as close to every day as possible. Not for very long, and even if there are no workers onsite, which happens. All contractors work multiple jobs. You don't want them to be exclusively dependent upon your job, unless you are very, very rich.

- **Be aware that in-person discussions make some things easier to explain.** Some subs won't be willing to try to describe something you can't see, or may not understand your directions if you phone them in. It's always easiest to resolve an issue when you're standing in front of it.

- **Show up at different times.** Don't call your subs to tell them that you're coming. Never act surprised at what they're doing.

- **Know that you don't have to micromanage the workers.** When there are problems—and there will be problems—deal with the person you hired, not someone *he's* hired, or worse, another sub who can't solve the problem. Let the fellow who's got the contract with you come up with the solution.

- **Give your subs the respect they deserve.** If your subs are doing a very good job, thank them—immediately and directly. If they don't deserve respect, be prepared to fire them.

And finally, this last caveat, from owner-builder Andrea Donnelly: "Try not to lose your temper, ever! But if you do, and you've started a battle, prepare to make peace." Recalls Andrea, "I once lost it with one of our subcontractors and they were ready to walk. My husband told me to make it up to them. I brought them some snacks and a case of beer, along with my apology, at the end of a very long day. It saved the project from problems that my temper had only exacerbated."

Pre-Building Worksheets

Indicate work completed and materials used for this section on the following pages. Check off each task as it is completed, or indicate N/A if the task does not apply to your project.

Pre-Building Worksheet

Work/Materials Description	Start/Complete (Estimated)	Sub or Contact (Name or Company)
☐ Check building ordinances		
☐ Cash on hand for pre-draw expenses		
☐ Construction docs reviewed		
☐ Construction docs revised/complete		
☐ Construction docs approved		
☐ Deed accessible		
☐ Title accessible and cleared		
☐ Title insurance		
☐ Driveway right-of-way approved		
☐ Builder's risk insurance		
☐ Well permit		
☐ Septic permit		
☐ Water test		
☐ Well inspected		
☐ Septic installed		
☐ Septic inspected		
☐ Permit applications (list)		
☐ Test hole for excavation		
☐ Approvals to obtain (list)		

	Start Date	Cost (Estimated)	Cost (Actual)	Complete Date	Ck. #	Lien Waiver

Pre-Building Worksheet

Work/Materials Description	Start/Complete (Estimated)	Sub or Contact (Name or Company)
☐ Permits obtained (list)		
☐ Sanitary facility ordered		
☐ Waste removal container ordered		
☐ Utility hookups ordered		
☐ Temp. electrical ordered		
☐ Temp. telephone ordered		
☐ Close construction loan (list all costs not previously listed)		

Start Date	Cost (Estimated)	Cost (Actual)	Complete Date	Ck. #	Lien Waiver

Notes

Clearing, Excavation, and Foundation

10

Now it's time for your lovely lot to be transformed by the large, loud machines that prepare the site for building. No matter how carefully you've planned, most owner-builders are not prepared for the noise, the rubble, and the major changes that land-moving equipment will make. So get ready, and when you're onsite with the earth-moving equipment going full tilt, *wear earplugs*. And if it's bug season, don't forget insect repellent!

The excavation and foundation for your house, hidden after they're finished, are critical points in the building process. You want them perfect, to set the stage for everything that's built on top of them. Expert subs make a big difference: seasoned excavators and foundation subs (sometimes the same person or company) are worth the premium you pay.

From the Home Team

Owner-builder Patti Garbeck designed a small house on her big Vermont parcel, with the idea that she'd be making a tiny human footprint. The reality of her own project took her by surprise. Says Patti, "Breaking ground was a big challenge. Seeing that huge equipment and the damage it could do, it didn't seem so low-impact. And of course, breaking ground in early May, when blackflies are at their worst, made me question my choice of location."

Clearing, Excavation, and Foundation Checklist

Use this checklist as a guide for this part of your schedule. Write the name of the person doing the work on the Contact line. When you've completed a task, check it off. Enter the information for each task on the worksheets at the end of this section. Check the dates against your master schedule (see Section 8) and the costs against your budget (see Section 1). Revise your schedule and budget as needed.

Work for This Phase	Contact

Clearing

☐ Silt barriers to protect against runoff installed _____

☐ Trees to be removed marked with orange tape _____

☐ Trees to be protected surrounded
   by orange polypropylene fencing _____

☐ Stumps and tree and brush waste removed _____

☐ Topsoil stripped and stockpiled _____
☐ Curb cut and construction phase driveway cleared _____

☐ Street number installed at curb _____

Excavation

☐ Batter boards installed and corners marked _____

☐ Full or partial cellar: hole excavated _____

☐ Blasting (if needed) permitted _____

☐ Blasting (if needed) completed _____

☐ Excavation for footings _____

☐ Footing pour scheduled _____

Foundation

☐ Footing forms installed _____

☐ Pre-pour footings inspection _____

   ___ Inspection passed

☐ Install footings _____

☐ Inspect footings _____

   ___ Inspection passed

☐ Foundation pour scheduled _____

☐ Set up for foundation walls _____

   ___ ICFs

   ___ Poured walls, forms

Work for This Phase	Contact
☐ Masonry block walls installed	_____
or	
☐ Slab preparation	_____
___ Base	
___ Insulation	
___ Poly barrier	
___ Rough-in plumbing and inspection	_____
___ Inspection passed	
☐ Pre-pour inspection for all requirements	_____
___ Inspection passed	
☐ Slab poured	_____
___ Other foundation work	
☐ Foundation inspected	_____
___ Inspection passed	
☐ Insect proofing	_____
☐ Waterproofing	_____
☐ Drainage system installed (if required)	_____
☐ Connections for water, underground utilities, and septic (if any) installed to foundation	_____
☐ Backfill	_____
☐ Foundation floor poured	_____

Clearing, Excavation, and Foundation Overview

Site preparation and the construction of a foundation are heavy-duty operations best done by experts. Because pouring foundations, and to some extent, excavation, are weather dependent, your start date may get pushed back if you have a rainy spell or extremely hot or freezing temperatures. Concrete sets best when the temperature is between 40°F and 80°F. If the temperature is lower, some foundation contractors will tent and heat a foundation hole to keep the concrete at the proper temperature, but this will add to your costs. A heat wave will also play havoc with pouring plans, which is why excavators and foundation contractors are busiest in the most temperate months. Line up your excavation and foundation subs early, but know that the weather may force you to be flexible on the start date.

Insulating concrete forms (ICFs) are one answer to the temperature problems (see "Foundation Walls" later in this section).

Keep in Mind

When your schedule gets stretched, alert subcontractors who will be affected by the delay—the ones next on the schedule. Most will hustle for fill-in work if you are held up. But they'll be *very* unhappy if you don't alert them.

Clearing

Here are a few pointers about clearing your property:

- Be *very sure* of your property lines before you do any clearing. If you damage a neighbor's property during the clearing process, you are liable.

- Inquire at the building department about your tree-cutting plans. Some towns, including mine, limit the amount of tree coverage on a lot that can be cleared for home construction.

- Have tree stumps hauled away, or chipped and removed. It's more expensive to haul tree waste away than to bury it, but the buried stumps further scar your landscape and will cost more to remove later on. Some towns prohibit stump burial.

- Conserve your topsoil. Good topsoil is expensive to buy, so don't waste what must be removed in the clearing, grading, and excavation of your site. Have the excavator retain the topsoil in a pile in an unused corner of the lot.

- If your road is wooded and lined with brush, it may be difficult for delivery trucks and subs to find your property. After the driveway is roughed-in, mark it with tape, a flag, a sign with your name, or the street number.

Excavation

Now it's time for the big, scary digging machines. Remember the children's book *Mike Mulligan and His Steam Shovel?* You get an up-close and personal look at the machine.

Marking the Corners

For the framing to be perfectly square, the foundation must be square as well. Usually, a builder will know how to site the house corners for excavation with a *transit,* a surveying instrument used for measuring vertical and horizontal angles. You can hire your surveyor to do this, or have the excavator do it, if he is experienced in this operation.

Because the equipment used to excavate is large and unwieldy, the corner markers are offset a few feet from the actual corners so that they are not disturbed by the equipment. This corner marking uses string and what are called *batter boards* (wood boards attached level to stakes) to mark the perimeter of the foundation and the level of the excavation.

If the corners are right, the foundation can be poured correctly, and the house will be square.

Blasting

If yours is a rocky area of the country, even a test hole made before you dig may miss the most expensive glitch in an excavation: ledge rock. The solution to this problem is blasting, which is expensive, usually requires special permits, and may foul wells in the blasting area.

If there's a chance you will need to blast, you can exclude blasting from the contract terms so you don't pay for what you won't need. Insert a contingency clause, and get the excavator to commit to a certain price per quantity of ledge rock removed. That way, you'll be aware up front of what the worst hit to your bottom line might be, without paying for it unless you need it.

From the Home Team

You might actually *want* to put your house on top of a foundation that's been blasted out of a ledge. This was the case for owner-builders Andrea and Jack Donnelly. "We could visualize the house at the top of the formations of ledge rock. So we budgeted for the extra expense. For this kind of work, you want the best, most experienced team you can find. Our blasting crew came from Pennsylvania, about six hours away, and they did a perfect job," recalls Andrea. She admits that the couple had no problem with the blast permit because theirs was the first house in their neighborhood. If your rocky lot is adjacent to existing houses and wells, blasting is a riskier business.

Foundation

Depending on soil conditions and the area of the country in which you live, you may have a full-height foundation or a partial-height foundation, or you may build on a concrete slab. Full foundations are the most expensive, but necessary because of soil and weather conditions in some parts of the country.

In his book *The Well-Built House* (see Appendix B), builder Jim Locke delves deeply into excavation and foundations in layman's terms. If you need more information, his book is a good place to start.

If you have approved drawings signed by a licensed architect or structural engineer, your excavator and foundation installer will dig and build to the plan.

Be sure to follow all the permitting and inspection procedures in your locale. Check with the local building department if you are unsure.

Footings

A structural engineer or licensed architect must check your plans, because buildings must have their structural and nonstructural weights (called *dead loads* and *live loads,* respectively) distributed safely over the structure and down to the ground.

Footings are the structural supports of a building that are in contact with undisturbed soil, below the point where the ground freezes (the *frost line*). Footings transmit the full load of the structure to the ground. Constructed of concrete, usually with steel reinforcement, footings are generally wider than the foundation wall. The footings' dimensions are generally based on the load (live and dead) of the structure.

Here's an illustration of a footing used in owner-builders Tom McNamara and Betsy Hagerty's foundation plan.

Sometimes you'll hear a contractor refer to these foundation elements as "footers." Their real name is footings, and yes, you need them.

Foundation Walls

A full or partial-height foundation will generally be built of masonry block or cast-in-place, poured concrete, generally strengthened with steel reinforcing bars (rebar).

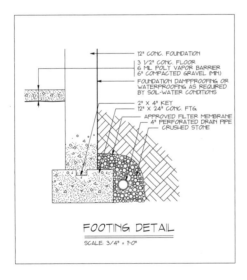

FOOTING DETAIL
SCALE: 3/4" = 1'-0"

12" CONC. FOUNDATION
3 1/2" CONC. FLOOR
6 MIL POLY VAPOR BARRIER
6" COMPACTED GRAVEL (MIN)
FOUNDATION DAMPPROOFING OR WATERPROOFING AS REQUIRED BY SOIL-WATER CONDITIONS
2" X 4" KEY
12" X 24" CONC. FTG.
APPROVED FILTER MEMBRANE
4" PERFORATED DRAIN PIPE
CRUSHED STONE

Footing detail. Tom and Betsy's house, sited on an existing footprint of an old house next to a lake, required footings such as the one pictured here.

© *Home Designing Service, Ltd.*

In recent years, insulating concrete forms (ICFs) have in some cases taken the place of an ordinary poured foundation, which is made by pouring the concrete into reusable forms that are removed after the concrete sets. Made of rigid plastic foam that holds the concrete while it dries and cures, ICFs stay in place after the concrete is poured. The forms provide thermal insulation, are lightweight, and result in a very energy-efficient, durable type of foundation construction.

Although ICFs are more expensive than pouring concrete into reusable forms, their insulating properties make it possible to pour concrete in warmer or colder temperatures.

Check with your architect or designer to determine whether ICFs might be a reasonable and affordable modification for your design.

From the Home Team

Foundations are quite dependent on the part of the country where you live and the nature of the soil. Owner-builder Cynde Clark has a 3-foot deep foundation under her most recent project—a beautiful, modestly sized home. Because of the high water table, the foundation could not go deeper. However, tradespeople hate crawl spaces and shallow basements because they are difficult to work in. Cynde alleviated this problem by installing a little trolley (the kind that auto mechanics use under your car) in her 3-foot-high basement. Everyone loves this solution when repairs are needed beneath the house.

Slab Foundations

Many homeowners forgo digging a cellar and build on a concrete slab; in fact, slabs are standard operating procedure in warmer climates. A slab is a less-expensive underpinning than an excavated, concrete-walled basement or crawl space, but it has its own requirements, including installing any pipe runs for plumbing before the slab is poured.

Installing Drainage

If water on your lot flows toward the house site, it should be controlled with drainpipes that direct water *away* from the house, mitigating potential structural or moisture problems. This is an inexpensive fix when you're building the house, but an expensive repair if you neglect it. The drainage system can be installed when the area around the foundation is exposed, then buried when the area is backfilled.

Insulation and Waterproofing

Damp basements cause a lot of problems, and these can be alleviated with waterproofing and insulation. Most local building codes require insulation and waterproofing of foundations. Be sure your plans fulfill these requirements, and consult your architect or structural engineers about the specifics.

Termite Proofing

Depending on your location, the soil below and around your foundation may need to be treated with some type of termite proofing. Some particularly hungry varieties of termites afflict homeowners in the southeastern United States. Application of insecticide requires a license, so be sure your sub is duly credentialed for the job.

Running Plumbing and Utility Lines into the House

Your mechanicals and utilities must enter the house, usually ganged together where you will dedicate a corner of the basement or a closet for pipes and wires to enter the house and then be dispersed throughout it. The trenches and utility line entry into the house should be planned for and/or installed when you prepare your foundation.

Backfill

Pushing the soil back into place against the foundation walls is ideally done in two stages. The area around the foundation is partially backfilled before the framing occurs. After the first floor decking is installed, providing more stability and strength to the base of your house, the excavator can return to complete backfilling.

Because partial backfilling makes getting into the house a little difficult—think ramps rigged from 2-by-4s and a lot of leaping—many subs will backfill all the way to the grade determined in the plans before the decking is installed for the first floor. This may turn out fine, but old-timers and purists believe that getting the deck on the house first prevents cracks from developing in the foundation.

Pouring the Foundation Floor

If the weather is cold, the foundation floor is best poured when the house is closed in and the temperature is most easily controlled. Again, concrete will only set and cure if the temperature is between 40°F and 80°F.

Clearing, Excavation, and Foundation Worksheets

Indicate work completed and materials used on the following pages.

Clearing, Excavation, and Foundation Worksheet

Work/Materials Description	Start/Complete (Estimated)	Sub or Contact (Name or Company)
Clearing		
☐ Silt barriers installed		
☐ Trees marked for removal		
☐ Trees fenced for protection		
☐ Clearing waste removed, including stumps		
☐ Topsoil stripped and stockpiled		
☐ Curb cut and temporary driveway cleared		
☐ Street number or other ID at curb		
Excavation		
☐ Batter boards installed and corners marked		
☐ Full or partial cellar hole excavated		
☐ Blasting permitted		
☐ Blasting completed		
☐ Excavation for footings		
☐ Footing pour scheduled		
Foundation		
☐ Footing forms installed		
☐ Inspect footings before pouring		
☐ Pass pre-pour footings inspection		
☐ Foundation pour scheduled		
☐ Set up for foundation walls		
____ ICF		
____ Poured walls, forms		

Start Date	Cost (Estimated)	Cost (Actual)	Complete Date	Ck. #	Lien Waiver

Clearing, Excavation, and Foundation Worksheet

Work/Materials Description	Start/Complete (Estimated)	Sub or Contact (Name or Company)
☐ Masonry block walls installed		
or		
☐ Slab prep		
___ Base		
___ Insulation		
___ Poly barrier		
___ Rough-in plumbing		
___ Rough-in plumbing inspect		
☐ Pre-pour inspection for all slab requirements		
___ Inspection passed		
☐ Foundation inspection		
___ Inspection passed		
☐ Insect proofing		
☐ Waterproofing		
☐ Drainage system installed (if required)		
☐ Connections to foundation		
___ Water		
___ Underground utilities		
___ Septic		
☐ Backfill		
☐ Foundation floor poured		

Start Date	Cost (Estimated)	Cost (Actual)	Complete Date	Ck. #	Lien Waiver

Notes

Walls and Roof: Framing and Sheathing

11

After the foundation is complete, your hole in the ground will suddenly begin to take the shape of a house. Framing proceeds at a pretty quick pace, and soon you'll see the "bones" of the home you've been dreaming about begin to create its silhouette.

Over the bones goes the sheathing, sheets of plywood that form the house's basic surfaces, including the floors. You can walk inside, a significant bit of progress. When the masons finish your chimneys—if they're part of the design—things are definitely shaping up.

Framing and Sheathing Checklist

Here's your quick checklist of what happens in this phase. Although most of the framing will be done by your framing subs, specific operations, such as installing roofing material, may be done by additional subcontractors. This list will remind you to give those other subs a call when the time for their work is approaching.

Work for This Phase	Contact
Framing	
☐ Lumber package	_____
☐ Fasteners	_____
☐ Sills	_____
☐ Girders	_____
☐ Lally columns	_____
☐ Check layout	_____
☐ Joists	_____
☐ Framing openings for stairs, other vertical passage	_____
☐ Subfloor (decking)	_____
☐ Check layout	_____
☐ Walls	_____
☐ Openings	_____

Work for This Phase	Contact

Window and Door Frames

- ☐ Sheathing (decking)   _____
- ☐ Figuring stair runs   _____
- ☐ Rough stairs   _____
- ☐ Interior partitions   _____
- ☐ Install and protect tubs and shower surrounds   _____
- ☐ Blocking   _____
- ☐ Upper floor framing   _____
- ☐ Sheathing (walls)   _____
- ☐ House wrap   _____

Roof Framing

- ☐ Framing (site-built)   _____
- ☐ Framing (truss)   _____
- ☐ Sheathing (roof frame)   _____
- ☐ Masonry chimneys   _____
- ☐ Flashing   _____
- ☐ Felt, membranes, and shingles   _____

Framing Your House

Your home's skeleton begins with your first lumber delivery; after your framing crew has set up their work site, things will proceed fairly quickly.

Your framing subs may have signed on for the whole job, or they may be joined by masons if you're building chimneys, and by roofing subs if you have a separate crew for this step.

Depending on the size of your house and how many floors there are, the framing and _drying-in_ process—getting the foundation out of the weather and closing in your building footprint with sheathed walls and a roof, will take from 10 days to several weeks. Your home's dimensions, the size of the crew, and of course the weather all influence your timeline.

Keep in Mind

How big should a framing crew be? Minimally, you need one person to cut lumber, one person to measure and install, and one person to carry the pieces from the cutting station to the installer. To go faster, you'll need a bigger crew. A team of five or six framing carpenters and helpers is probably ideal.

The Lumber Package

Dimensional lumber is the material of choice for building homes. Check your delivery to make sure that you received everything you ordered, comparing your purchase order against the stacks.

It's best to have the material delivered in stages, as unused lumber should be piled off the ground and covered, to protect it from ground moisture and bad weather. The less lumber you store for an extended period, the better its condition when it becomes part of your house.

Bundles are often tied with strapping, and most carpenters encourage keeping the strapping intact until you need to break into a bundle.

Choosing Good Wood

Many building professionals bemoan the condition of what's considered to be framing-quality lumber. If you pick up a 2-by-4 and sight down its length, you can see if it's straight, or whether it's got defects that make it unacceptable. These imperfections include a bend on the face (wide) side, called *cupping;* edge curves, called *crooks;* or knots that run clear through, which weaken the wood.

When you have your lumber take-off ready, you can go to the lumberyard and select your own; owner-builder and professional carpenter Patti Garbeck recommends this strategy.

Pro Know-How

Architect Mac Rood advises buying your lumber in 16- or 18-foot pieces, and cutting studs by halving the longer material. "Generally, because imperfections are easier to sight on the longer pieces, the lumber in these lengths is better." Just remember that you'll need a bigger area for your pile, and a more generous cutting area for your subs. A 16- or 18-footer has a wide swing!

Fasteners

You don't need to have a debate about fasteners for your frame. Nails that are vulnerable to rust are a bad idea for any project exposed to weather. Specify *hot-dipped* galvanized nails. *Common* nails with the hot-dipped galvanized coating are usually used for the framing of a house. Browse through Appendix B for resources on these indispensable little bits.

Sills: The Frame Begins

The first part of your home's wood frame is a horizontal single layer of framing wood known as the *sill* (also called a *sill plate*), which is attached to the foundation with hefty fasteners, called *anchor bolts*. Because most foundations are not perfectly level around the entire perimeter, this is the framer's opportunity to even things out. *Level* and *plumb* (perfectly straight, horizontally and vertically) are the rules of a good frame. The framing crew will often insert wood shims (thin pieces of cedar shingle material) to close the small gaps that may be apparent at certain spots in the perimeter. The crew will cut the shims flush with the sill later in the process—they won't stick out at the end! They will also create a seal between foundation and sill with an insulating product, usually a spray foam.

Keep in Mind

Because sills are the layer of wood closest to the ground, most builders use moisture-resistant, pressure-treated wood. The first generation of pressure-treated wood, which used arsenic, was banned for residential use in 2004. The alternative products require special considerations; see Appendix B for more information.

Girders and Lally Columns

Horizontal spans greater than 10 or 12 feet usually require extra support in the frame of your house. This extra support is provided by the use of one or more *girders*. A girder is a large support beam of greater size than other horizontal pieces of the frame. Sometimes the girder will be a beam custom-made of engineered lumber, or a super-sized member made of multiple 2-by-10s or 2-by-12s glued together. If your house is more than 20-feet wide or deep, its frame will usually require a girder.

The girder is usually set on pipe columns, also known as lally columns (metal pipes filled with concrete) that rest on substantial footings spanning the basement or foundation.

Joists

Joists form a grid that supports your house. Depending on your frame specs, the joists will be attached level to the girders with special metal joist hangers, or they will be nailed on top of the girders.

As the grids of your home come together, you will see the regular spacing between joists (horizontal) and then between studs (vertical). Until recently, standard building practice was a frame built 16 inches on center, meaning that the framing pieces were installed 16 inches apart, from the center of one piece to the center of the next one. A more recently popular standard in residential building is 24 inches on center for studs; 2-by-6 studs are used instead of 2-by-4 to allow for thicker insulation and better energy performance. The heftier studs mean that overall stability and frame strength are not sacrificed for energy savings.

Layout Check

The placement of all pieces of the frame—horizontal and vertical—is critical to the integrity of the building. That's why your framing crew will study the plans repeatedly, and why they constantly wield the compact metal extension rulers attached to their waistbands. Those quarters and eighths of an inch really matter. Learn to use the builder's measuring tools yourself, particularly the level and the measuring tape.

The layout check is part of the checklist for this section. Walk around with your subs and have them show you where things are going. This is the time for changes if you notice anything in the layout that doesn't work. Although changes will still cost, they will cost much less.

Pro Know-How

Whether you're experienced or a GC beginner, you should know that every contractor owns his own tools; borrowing is frowned upon. Says architect Mac Rood, "If you're going to be a GC, *have your own set of tools, and know how to use them.*" Although you may not need to learn to run a table saw, or use some of the other big power tools, having your own measuring instruments, hand saw, and other common items should be a given. You will more quickly earn the respect of your subs if you follow this simple rule. See Appendix C for a list of basic tools.

Framing for Stair Openings and Other Vertical Passages

Wherever there's a stair, you'll need an opening in the framing for the floor where it begins and framing above it where the stair reaches the next story.

Stairs are tricky; measuring must be painstaking so that the *stringer*—the "step" part of the stair that supports the treads—is cut with steps of equal height and treads of equal width. Otherwise, the stairway will be a non-code-worthy hazard.

After the stairs are figured and the walls are up, the crew will most likely install temporary stairs where the permanent staircase will be built in during the finishing process.

Other openings in your horizontal layout will include masonry chimneys, which will rise from the foundation up through the roof. Other vertical spaces may include chases for piping and wiring, or an opening between floors to accommodate an elevator or laundry chute.

When laying out joists for the floor frame, the framing crew will install headers wherever there's an opening. A *header* is a framing member that runs perpendicular to adjacent framing (the joists in horizontal framing; the studs in vertical framing).

Rim Joists

When the joists for the first floor are all installed, nailed to the sills and the girders, the framing crew will install the rim joists, which form the perimeter of the base of the house's frame. The best, straightest boards are the ones for this job. Remember, level and plumb.

Inspections

Be sure that you call the building department in advance for any inspections required by your municipality during the framing process. This includes any masonry or chimney inspections.

Sheathing (Decking)

When the support structure is firmly in place, the first floor is covered with plywood decking. Your first steps on your first floor will be very exciting. Things are coming together!

Walls

Now the crew will mark off the openings in the walls for windows and doors. Plans will be studied carefully, alignment of window and door openings checked and rechecked.

Most crews will build the wall on the deck, and raise it when it's complete, bracing it with 2-by-4s until it is firmly nailed in place.

The outside of the walls is sheathed with plywood. Some crews cut out the rough openings for windows and doors before the sheathing goes on. Others sheathe the wall and then cut out the openings. Either way, the important thing is that the sheathing be well fastened and plumb when raised into position.

Interior Partitions

Some crews like to build the walls before framing interior partitions. However, any load-bearing partition walls will go in before the second floor is framed.

Blocking

Throughout your house, you have probably planned a number of elements that must be attached firmly to the walls: kitchen cabinets, wall-hung bath fixtures, towel bars, etc.

To give these house parts a firm attachment to the body of the house, your framing carpenters will need to insert pieces of 2-by-4s between joists at the proper height for the wall-hung features. This is called *blocking*.

Most good framing crews will think of this step, but if they don't, remind them of this small but very helpful part of the house frame.

Oversized Tubs and Shower Enclosures

Although it's not yet rough-in time, if you're planning to use shower enclosures or over-sized tubs that will not fit through door openings when the interior walls and doorways are in place, they will need to be put in place before all the interior partitions are constructed. Make sure you order them and take delivery at the right time; if complex piping will be involved later, you may want the plumber to come in at this time to confirm placement.

The surfaces of tubs and enclosures may be vulnerable to scratches and stains from everything going on around them, so protect them with heavy plastic wrapping.

House Wrap

When the walls of the house are framed, the crew will usually apply building wrap that functions as a weather-resistant barrier, protecting the walls from the elements. This is stapled carefully to the plywood sheathing, as tears and holes defeat the purpose. This layer goes under all the trim and the finish siding (shingles, clapboard, stucco, and so on).

Upper Story Floors and Walls

These will go up in the same way as the first floor: joists, vertical opening framing, sheathing (decking), walls, wall sheathing.

The Roof Frame

Depending on your plans, your roof may be a simple one, or have many ridges, valleys, and dormers in its design.

Many new homes do not have site-built roofs, and are instead constructed with *trusses*—prefabricated, triangular-shaped structures that form the frame of the roof. These are usually put into place with a crane. These are less expensive than a crew-built roof frame, but their design usually precludes the use of the space beneath the roof ridge as an attic or living space.

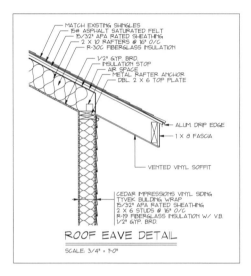

ROOF EAVE DETAIL

SCALE: 3/4" = 1'-0"

Eave section detail: The requirements for framing and insulating a roof are often very detailed, and usually get their own drawing in a set of construction documents. This illustration shows how the wall and roof come together; the part that projects beyond the wall is known as the eave.

© *Rick Thompson, Architect*

Roof Sheathing

When the frame is constructed, the framers will apply plywood sheathing, which will provide a base for the roofing material and the various protective layers that are part of the roof.

If you are going to have a masonry chimney, this is the point at which the mason will build it, up from the basement footings through the roof.

After the roof is decked with its layer of plywood, further protective layers include a *drip edge*, which does what its name implies: it helps water drip off the edge of the roof and away from the walls of the house.

Metal *flashing* is applied to all the joints in the roof. Copper flashing is the preferred (and the most expensive) material; it will outlast any roof and need not be reapplied every time a roof is re-shingled. Aluminum is a much cheaper flashing material.

In areas with snowy winters, building codes may require a *snow and ice membrane* beneath the roofing material. This fairly expensive membrane is nonetheless far less costly than the damage water trapped on your roof by ice dams will cause. Ice dams often occur in early winter freeze and thaw cycles, when the water trapped by iced-in gutters works its way under shingles and into the walls. It's a mess and a pain to repair.

Over this protective coating goes a layer of *roofing felt,* also known as tarpaper.

Shingles are the top layer. The least-expensive are three-tabbed asphalt shingles, followed upward on the pricing scale by various types of asphalt coverings known as architectural shingles. These are designed to give the roof some added dimension, replicating more expensive materials. Architectural shingles also have a higher wear rating, lasting up to 40 years.

Keep in Mind

Asphalt shingles are vulnerable to heat, so don't fry them! If you have bundles waiting to be used, protect them from the sun and other weather with a plastic tarp. Keep them in a sheltered situation if possible.

The higher-priced choices include wood, metal, tile, and slate. Although expensive, many people find these materials beautiful and worth their cost.

A Complete Shell

Even without its roofing material, your sheathed and wrapped house has taken shape. When the house is framed, you'll have a sense of its form, though it's still a long way from completion.

Keep up with your paperwork and make sure your checklist is finished.

Then it's time for openings.

Framing and Sheathing Worksheets

Indicate work done and materials used on the following pages. Check off each task as it is completed, or indicate N/A if the task does not apply to your project. Because lumber quantities and types, as well as roofing materials, will vary with the job, there are plenty of blank spaces for you to enter materials that are specific to your project.

Framing and Sheathing Worksheet

Work/Materials Description	Start/Complete (Estimated)	Sub or Contact (Name or Company)
Framing		
☐ Lumber package		
Delivery dates—multiple (list):		
☐ Fasteners (list):		
☐ Tubs/showers for early install		
☐ House wrap		
☐ Framing inspection scheduled		
☐ Inspection pass		

Start Date	Cost (Estimated)	Cost (Actual)	Complete Date	Ck. #	Lien Waiver

Framing and Sheathing Worksheet

Work/Materials Description	Start/Complete (Estimated)	Sub or Contact (Name or Company)
Roof Framing		
☐ Trusses (if used)		
☐ Masonry chimney		
☐ Chimney inspections scheduled		
☐ Inspections pass [may be multiples]		
Roof Coverings		
☐ Drip edge		
☐ Flashing		
☐ Membrane		
☐ Roofing felt		
☐ Roofing material		
Delivery dates—multiple (list):		

	Start Date	Cost (Estimated)	Cost (Actual)	Complete Date	Ck. #	Lien Waiver

Notes

Windows and Doors, Exterior Siding

12

The form of your house is now apparent, but its personality becomes clearer when the windows and doors are in place. After the siding is installed, you'll have something close to the finished product.

Now is the time to check level and plumb for all the installed openings; use a good level (one *you* own). Difficulty opening and closing windows and doors are the sad result of poor installation. Don't worry if your subcontractor takes time to do it right. This is a place where installers need to sweat the details.

Windows, Doors, and Siding Checklist

Check off each step when it's done. Some things, like finish coats of paint on trim, may be done later; just be sure that all the details are completed before the subcontractor gets the final payment.

Work for This Phase	Contact
Window and Door Installation	
☐ Schedule window and door delivery	_____
☐ Check all deliveries for quantities, accuracy	
☐ Flashing	_____
☐ Trim	_____
☐ Paint or prime	_____
☐ Check level and plumb	_____
☐ Door clearances okay	_____
☐ Window/door hardware	_____
Siding Installation	
☐ Schedule delivery	_____
☐ Siding delivery check order	_____
☐ Install siding trim	_____
☐ Install siding	_____

Just-in-Time Delivery

Windows and exterior doors are expensive, so make sure that you receive no more windows than you can install or securely store at one time.

Keep in Mind

When your windows and doors are delivered, check sizes, model numbers, features, and options (cladding finishes inside and outside, hardware finishes, screens or glass energy panels, and so on). Be onsite when deliveries are made and supervise placement and storage of the materials until they are installed.

Window and Door Installation

Doors and windows are called *openings* because they open the building to the outside. However, they must also *close* securely.

Good installation makes your windows and doors work smoothly and well. Windows or doors that leak heated or air-conditioned air are energy guzzlers. You want your openings to be watertight, and as airtight as possible. First, you must have good products. Then, a level and plumb installation, plus the right weather stripping and insulating materials, will ensure smooth operation and energy efficiency.

As a GC, you approve all installations. Check window and door installations with a good carpenter's level. After the openings are closed in with siding, trim, and finishes, it will be a big and expensive job to set them straight. If you are retaining your architect to help you supervise the construction process, this is a good time for a site visit. Ask the architect to come as the installation begins, to check that his specs and instructions are being followed correctly.

Flashing

Metal flashing that diverts water away from the windows and doors is a must, unless you live in extremely arid conditions. Water infiltration, which may go undetected for some time, can ruin your windows as well as your house. A window or door section in your plans or the installer instructions that come with the windows should show a flashing detail for the installation. Make sure that all the windows and doors are installed according to specifications and instructions.

Trim

Most windows are delivered with their exterior trim attached.

After the window is fitted into its rough opening, leveled and flat (plumb), it can be nailed in. The installers—your carpentry crew, unless you hired a window and door company—will use shims to make the windows absolutely level in their rough openings.

Painting and Finishing

You may have purchased windows and doors that are already primed and painted, or stained and sealed (in the case of wood doors). Or your windows may have some type of weatherproof exterior cladding and be finished on the inside, or primed and ready for painting during the finish work. If this is the case, then all you have to do is the installation.

If you have new windows that are not preprimed, however, all the raw wood surfaces that will disappear after installation should be primed before installation. This is known as *backpriming* and protects hidden wood from moisture damage due to leaks. It's rare to purchase new windows that aren't preprimed, but know to check.

Hardware

Hardware for doors and windows is installed after the openings are in place. Take special care with the decorative plates and latches of main entry doors, because lots of materials and equipment will be moving through these openings.

Keep in Mind

The beautiful finishes on new door handles and latches are not immune to scratches and dings. Protect surfaces with masking tape or another cover-up until you're ready for the final inspection and move-in.

Finished Floor Heights

Right now, you've only got a layer of plywood sheathing on your floors; the finished floors will be installed later. Be sure there is room for all the underlayments and flooring—wood, tile, stone, carpet and padding, or whatever you choose—when the door swings. Make sure this allowance is made when each door, including sliding doors, is installed.

Siding

You may choose to have your carpentry crew install siding while the rough-ins (see Section 13) are going on inside the house. With a tight schedule, this is often a good idea. Remember, however, that you will have to watch all the action, inside and out. You may need to make time to be on the site for longer periods than you have been up to this point.

Depending on where you live, you may have selected wood clapboards, cedar shingles, various forms of vinyl cladding, cement fiber shingles, brick or stone facing, stucco, or something else for siding. The installation of each type of material has its own specific requirements. Talk with your subs and read up on your type of siding, so that you can be aware of the challenges of the material you've picked.

Siding and Trim Materials

Many people wouldn't think of using nontraditional siding materials such as vinyl and composites for cladding and trim boards. However, improvements in synthetics, which deeply cut the costs of long-term maintenance, have made them popular with many owner-builders. Exterior cladding is so expensive and labor intensive that many prefer options requiring less maintenance over the long haul.

In fact, the latest generation of vinyl products so closely resembles its wood counterparts that it's difficult to tell the difference unless you're just a nose away from the side of the house.

In any case, your siding is a personal choice that you base on your budget and preferences.

Installing Siding Trim

Trim pieces are attached to the house before the siding goes up, as the siding will butt up against the cornice, the corner boards, or the pilasters that flank the front door. Check your specifications and consult with your subs to see whether felt (tar paper) needs to be installed under trim to protect against leakage between siding and trim. The gap between the two elements is often filled with caulk after installation. Different materials will have different weatherizing requirements.

Installing Siding

As with the roof, installing the siding is a painstaking process. Not only must the result provide a neat and finished appearance; it is also the top layer of protection for your house against the elements.

Keep an eye on the installation to ensure that the material's visual appeal and protective capacity is uncompromised.

From the Home Team

Here are some pointers from owner-builder Siobhan Daggett-Terenzi, who did her own siding installation: "Choose a siding material with a good warranty. Ask your dealer for local homes that have the same material and color you've chosen. If you can't see a sample in place, try to get larger samples of the material so you can look at them at the site, in different light at different times of the day. One of the trickiest parts of the job is aligning the courses of siding around the outside corners so they'll match on the inside corners. Pay attention to the way that installers cut and crimp the material under window sills, and how they create the layout so that the soffit meets the siding in a visually appealing way."

Next Steps

It's time to set your speed dial, as roughing-in the mechanical systems comes next. You'll be scheduling subs and watching as the walls of your house fill with all the pipes and wires that will make you comfortable when it's done. Right now, these things are about to keep you on your toes!

Windows, Doors, and Siding Worksheets

Indicate work completed and materials used on the following pages.

Windows, Doors, and Siding Worksheet

Work/Materials Description	Start/Complete (Estimated)	Sub or Contact (Name or Company)
Windows		
☐ Flashing		
☐ Trim		
☐ Hardware		
☐ Installation		
☐ Prime (if required)		
Doors, Exterior		
☐ Flashing		
☐ Trim		
☐ Hardware		
☐ Installation		
Siding		
☐ Material		
☐ Trim		
☐ Fasteners		
All Materials		
☐ Siding		
☐ Installation		

	Start Date	Cost (Estimated)	Cost (Actual)	Complete Date	Ck. #	Lien Waiver

Notes

Rough-Ins, Closing Interior Walls

13

Everything that goes between the exterior sheathing and the finished interior walls will be installed in this phase. Plan on making lots of decisions that will be difficult and costly to alter later. It's not ironic that they call this rough-in work; it will be rough on you, too!

All manner of pipe and wire will be going through your walls. The sequence starts with the largest conduits: the duct runs of your HVAC (heating, ventilation, and air conditioning) system. Next come the plumbing conduits: supply lines, plus DWV (drain, waste, and vent) runs. Then come the electrical wires. Finally, the modern amenities—security, central vacuum, audio/visual, telephone, cable, or multimedia systems—take their places.

Although ideally each trade—HVAC, plumber, electrical contractor, etc.—will come in, do the work, and leave as the next subcontractor shows up, the process is seldom quite so orderly. In addition to the subs, the inspectors of all these systems will have to sign off before the insulation and drywall go in. There will be a lot of noise, people, equipment, and material to orchestrate. As GC, this will be your most challenging time.

Roughing-In Through Closing Walls Checklist

This checklist has lots of items. Be sure you've gotten every task done before moving on. Pay careful attention to scheduling and inspections.

Work for This Phase	Contact
HVAC Rough-In	
☐ Walk-through to check layout	_____
☐ Installation	_____
☐ Schedule inspection	_____
☐ Inspection	_____
☐ HVAC rough-in inspection passed	_____
Plumbing Rough-In	
☐ Walk-through to check layout	_____
☐ Installation	_____
☐ Schedule inspection	_____
☐ Inspection	_____
☐ Plumbing rough-in inspection passed	_____
Electrical Rough-In	
☐ Walk-through to check layout	_____
☐ Installation	_____
☐ Schedule inspection	_____
☐ Inspection	_____
☐ Electrical rough-in inspection passed	_____
Other Rough-Ins	
☐ Phone	_____
☐ Central vac	_____
☐ Cable	_____
☐ Intercom	_____
☐ Security	_____
☐ Multimedia	_____
☐ Other Smart House technology	_____
	_____
	_____
	_____

Work for This Phase	Contact

Walk-Throughs for Other Rough-Ins

- ☐ _____   _____
- ☐ _____   _____
- ☐ _____   _____
- ☐ _____   _____
- ☐ _____   _____

Additional Rough-In Inspections

- ☐ _____   _____
- ☐ _____   _____
- ☐ _____   _____
- ☐ _____   _____
- ☐ _____   _____

Insulation Installation

- ☐ Installation   _____
- ☐ Schedule inspection   _____
- ☐ Inspection passed   _____

Drywall Installation

- ☐ Drywall hanging   _____
- ☐ Schedule inspection   _____
- ☐ Inspection passed   _____
- ☐ Drywall taping   _____
- ☐ Drywall finishing   _____
- ☐ Clean-up before finish phase   _____

Walk-Through with Your Subs

Before the subcontractors start installing ductwork, pipes, and wires, you should be on the same page about the layout. You want to make sure your fixtures, receptacles, heating and cooling vents, hard-wired security systems, and multimedia all wind up where you visualized them. If things change a bit in the actual installation, you should agree that the changes are preferable.

The walk-through may reveal places where one system bumps into another. Perhaps a duct will be in the way of a planned pipe. A walk-through with each sub and a copy of the plans will let you find the problem areas before you find your subs toe to toe, glaring at each other because one's work is in the path of the other's.

Spending Your Allowances

Once the mechanical systems are going into the walls, you must start deciding on, and ordering, any fixtures and fittings that will be needed for the finish work. If you hadn't made all your decisions when you made up your budget, you had to leave allowances for some items.

Make your decisions now. You don't want to make up your mind when your subs are ready to install the light fixtures or faucets. You also don't want to overspend your allowances. Also, if your budget has been creeping into negative territory—you've come in over budget on certain steps—you can step down the price of some elements, and perhaps postpone others. The finished basement, garage, or attic, for example, can wait for the future. Your priorities are completing the living spaces, keeping everything code-worthy for the building inspector (and you), and getting a house that you can live in.

HVAC Rough-In

Forced-air systems account for about two thirds of heating systems installed in the United States. Only in the Northeast are hydronic (gas- or oil-heated water or steam) systems more popular.

Forced-air systems are (1) less expensive than hydronic systems and (2) use ducts that can also circulate cool air from a central air-conditioning unit. With a forced-air system, you can also install the air conditioning later, without having to cut into the walls for new ductwork.

Because the heating, ventilation, and cooling of your home require the largest conduits through the walls, this is the first rough-in work to go in.

Staying on Schedule

The most important thing is keeping all your rough-in subs in the loop. If the HVAC sub is delayed, this pushes back everyone's schedule. If you don't keep the other subs informed, they may not be ready when you are; they may have moved on to their next job, pushing you back further in the line.

As an owner-builder GC who does not give subs regular employment, you have to have patience and be able to juggle things. Every ounce of your diplomatic skills will be needed to keep the subs working steadily. Despite your best intentions, you will probably have two or more subs at work in your walls at once; as well, you will have days when nothing gets done because of delays and schedule glitches.

Keep your cool, and keep going. Use those breaks in the action to check work, get your files in order, and do other administrative tasks.

Pro Know-How

Eyrich Stauffer, a professional woodworker and teacher at Yestermorrow Design Build School in Vermont, gives this advice: "Ask your subs what they need, and show interest in them as human beings. Go pick up stuff for them when it makes sense. And never underestimate the power of coffee, donuts, or a case of beer at the end of a demanding workweek. These small things go a long way to make good relationships with your subs."

Plumbing Rough-In

The plumber arrives to connect every location that uses fresh water to its supply (municipal water or your well), and also to provide conduits for draining wastewater, as well as vents so that the two never mix.

The rough work will determine the finish work; after walls are up, it's tough to move supply and waste lines. If your architect has included a plumbing layout in the plan, it will be easier to make sure everything is in the right spot. If not, your walk-through is critical, and another juncture at which your architect's eye will be helpful.

Pitfalls here are too-large holes drilled through critical support members of your frame, a big no-no. Pipes must also be protected from fasteners that will be used to hang the interior walls and install the trim. Protective plates at baseboard level will deflect nails and screws from your expensive piping system.

Electrical Rough-In

As with the plumber's rough work, the electrician's rough-ins will locate all the controls and fixtures in your house. Without the walls in place, it may be tough to visualize your chandeliers, sconces, wall switches, etc. Walk through the house with your family before you walk through with the sub. Make a list of the locations of the various switches, receptacles, and fixtures in each room, plus your questions. Then you can resolve your questions with your architect, if you're using one, and the electrical contractor.

Protective plates on studs the wiring snakes through are another safety measure put in place before walls go up. A good electrical inspector will notice any gaps, but as the installation progresses, you should watch as well.

Be sure that your electrician identifies the location of each circuit on a chart, which is usually glued to the inside of the electrical panel door in your utility room or basement. Tracing the locations that match the breakers is a time-consuming pain later on.

Other System Rough-Ins

Conduits for audio-visual, security, phone, central vacuum, cable television, and Internet access are also much easier to install when walls are open.

Is your fondest wish for a flat-screen television over the fireplace? A computer-controlled, whole-house audio/visual system? Maybe your budget is telling you no right now, but you dread the thought of opening your walls and snaking wires a couple years down the road.

Even if you are not ready for the full systems, having wires in place for future installations is a lot easier now than post-insulation and drywall. If you are contemplating hard-wired amenities now or in the future, get your systems pre-wired now.

Inspections for Rough-Ins

As each sub nears the completion of his work, you need to line up the inspector for that mechanical system.

A few days before each sub is finished, call the building department or the appropriate inspector and line up the inspection.

Keep in Mind

You may have to wait for the inspector, but he doesn't have time to wait for you. If your sub won't be finished by the time of your appointment, call the inspector with enough notice so that he doesn't waste time, gas, and energy on a futile inspection. This is not the way to win friends in building departments!

A Failed Inspection

Everyone hates when this happens, but sometimes it does. If you've hired reputable professionals, the infraction is usually small and easily remedied. If the problem is serious, you may have to fire the sub and find another contractor. But ideally your sub can fix the problem, and you can make another appointment.

Do not let this glitch make you lose your cool, particularly in front of your subcontractors. Deal with the problem calmly. And don't forget to phone the next subs. No insulation can be installed until all the work inside the walls passes inspection.

Insulation and Inspection

A professional insulation installation constitutes a big part of your home's energy efficiency. No matter how energy-smart your HVAC installation, without good insulation the savings in energy leak away.

The building code in your area will require certain minimum *R-values*—the capacity of the material to impede heat flow—for floors, walls, and roof. That's why many building departments require insulation inspections.

Your insulation installers will probably work very fast. But they will carefully insulate around the electrical boxes for receptacles and switches—a big source of cold air inflow and heat out-go. If you have any questions about what a code-worthy installation looks like, call your building department.

Although blown-in cellulose and spray foam have become popular as insulating products, fiberglass insulating batts are still the default choice of most builders. The batts are available in a number of R-values (the higher the R-value number, the better the insulating capacity), and insulating with batts is still the least expensive approach to insulation.

When the insulation installation passes inspection, you will be ready for the drywall installers.

Installing Drywall

Now it's time for the musclemen of the sub crews—the drywall installers. This crew hustles around with 4-foot-by-8-foot drywall panels, each one weighing about 70 pounds. They cut the stuff to fit, screw it to the wall studs, and work faster than you can imagine. It's a tough, dusty, and dirty job, and even if you're handy with a hammer and a screw gun, this work is best left to the pros.

Keep in Mind

With homes more tightly insulated than ever, you'll want to make sure that moisture-resistant drywall is installed in the damp locations in your house—specifically, the bathrooms. For better moisture protection in areas that are frequently wet, such as shower stalls and bathtubs, use *waterproof* drywall. Moisture can penetrate grout and get behind ceramic tile, dampening drywall that is merely resistant to water; then the problems with wall degradation and mold can start. Just as you did with walls subject to outside weather conditions, use hot-dipped galvanized fasteners in damp and wet locations. If nongalvanized fasteners rust through, your drywall can separate from the studs.

Drywall Inspection

Drywall goes up quickly, so as soon as the crew shows up, see if they can gauge when they'll complete the job. Then schedule the drywall inspection (if required). After the installation passes the inspection, the tapers can come in.

Drywall Taping

Sealing and smoothing the seams between sheets of drywall requires three applications of joint compound (also known as mud). The first coat goes on with drywall tape that physically closes the gap between the sheets of drywall. Inside corners are closed with drywall tape; outside corners—vulnerable to chipping and breaking—are covered with a metal edge before the compound is applied.

Getting good coverage of all the joints requires a bit of artistry. A bad taping job will show through paint, especially if your finish paint has any sheen. Although some drywall installers also employ tapers, these are very different jobs and will most likely be done by two different crews.

Examine the taped and smoothed walls in bright light, and correct any flaws before the final cleanup.

Taping and compound applications raise large quantities of fine dust. This dust can be extremely irritating to the human respiratory system. Some drywall installers don't use masks and goggles, but their lungs will pay the price later. You should wear a good-quality dust-filtering mask when you're onsite.

Clean-Up Time

It's exciting to finish the rough-ins, and finally have walls, ceilings, and distinct partitions between rooms. The house is shaping up, inside and out.

After all the subs finish, it's a good time to clean up. Sweeping and vacuuming before the finish work starts gives the next round of subs a nice, clean canvas to work with. You may want to save money on the cleaning service, and do the sweeping and dusting yourself. It will give you a chance to take a closer look at everything that's done so far, and catch any details that need mending before you go forward.

Roughing-In Through Closing Walls Worksheets

Indicate work completed and materials used on the following pages. Check off each task as it is completed, or indicate N/A if the task does not apply to your project.

Roughing-In Through Closing Walls Worksheet

Work/Materials Description	Start/Complete (Estimated)	Sub or Contact (Name or Company)
HVAC Rough-In		
☐ Materials		
☐ Labor		
Plumbing Rough-In		
☐ Materials		
☐ Labor		
Electrical Rough-In		
☐ Materials		
☐ Labor		
Other Rough-In		
☐		
☐		
☐		
☐		
Insulation		
☐ Materials		
☐ Labor		
Drywall Hanging		
☐ Materials		
☐ Labor		
Drywall Taping		
☐ Materials		
☐ Labor		
☐ Cleanup		

	Start Date	Cost (Estimated)	Cost (Actual)	Complete Date	Ck. #	Lien Waiver

Notes

Outside Structures: Garages, Porches, and Decks

14

Unless these elements are integral to the building envelope, the outdoor living spaces—porches and decks—and the garage can be built after the house is closed in and interior work has begun. Waiting to add these elements makes them options for cutting if your spending has exceeded your budget. Although having everything you want in place is the ideal, these outdoor living spaces can be added on later.

Outside Structures Checklist

Since outside structures get installed according to what works in your schedule and budget, check off each entry at whatever point these tasks are completed. Use N/A (not applicable) for items you will not be building.

Work for This Phase	Contact
Garages	
☐ Foundation	_____
Type: ___ Slab	
___ Crawl	
___ Full	
☐ Inspection(s)	_____
☐ Frame	_____
☐ Roof	_____
☐ Framing inspection	_____
☐ Openings installed	_____
☐ Rough-ins for plumbing/electrical	_____
☐ Mechanicals inspection	_____
☐ Finishes	_____
☐ Garage door opener installed	_____
☐ Shelving, accessories installed	_____
☐ Final inspection	_____

Work for This Phase	Contact
Porches	
☐ Footings	_____
☐ Inspection (foundation elements)	_____
pass ____	
☐ Support structure	_____
☐ Framing	_____
☐ Roof	_____
☐ Inspection (framing elements)	_____
pass ____	
☐ Finishes	_____
Decks	
☐ Support structure	_____
☐ Framing	
☐ Inspection (deck frame)	
pass ____	
☐ Railing	_____
☐ Finishes	_____

Building the Garage

The garage has evolved from its once-lowly status as a glorified shed at the back of a lot. Many thousands of dollars are often invested in a building that shelters multiple vehicles, as well as outdoor equipment, tools, out-of-season storage, and sometimes a small accessory apartment or guest quarters.

As long as you build a sturdy and code-worthy structure that is large enough to handle multiple functions, you can add finish details such as fireproof drywall, heat, integrated shelving and storage, or an office, work, or guest space at a later date. Sometimes these "accessory uses" require zoning variances and special permits, and you may not want to jump through these legal hoops at the moment. After all, your *house* needs to be finished. Keep in mind, however, that any big plans down the road must be permitted in the structure you put up now. Check this out with your building department.

Also, find out the inspection requirements for your outside structures. Garages and decks have had to be taken down when the correct procedure for inspection was not followed.

Keep in Mind

To economize, many builders frame the garage roof with trusses instead of a site-built frame. This makes the construction less expensive, but eliminates the loft space under the roof. If you're planning on storing heavy items in this space, in addition to a site-built roof frame, you'll need a heavier supporting structure, including a run of columns for a large floor span. Such extra framing will add to the cost of your garage.

Garage Foundation

Although rare, a full-height foundation under the garage can provide space for recreation or cool, dark storage. Some owners use the space beneath the garage for a soundproofed home theater. Wine collectors might find it ideal for cellaring their stash.

Most garages are built on slabs, which are subject to inspection, just as the house's supports are. Follow your building department's guidance on the inspection schedule.

Garage Framing

Standard garage doors (for a single car) are 9 feet wide by 7 feet tall. However, if you've got a pickup, large van, or SUV, you may need more room to maneuver. Be sure of what you need before the openings are framed in. If the approach to the garage is not a straight path, you may need more width to accommodate the angle necessary to turn in or back out.

Rough-Ins

Although most people need only lights and sufficient wiring to operate the garage door opener and electric tools, you may have bigger plans for your garage. Be sure to include sufficient circuits for your plans for the space.

Most garages are not plumbed, but some people like the convenience of a utility sink or an exterior hose bib for garden chores or washing the car. In colder regions, you may want to put the water shut-off in the main house so you can drain the pipes and shut off the water supply during frost season.

Garage Finishes

Most garages are finished with the same siding and roofing materials as the house. Because the garage is proportionally smaller than the house, trim pieces may be scaled slightly smaller.

Keep in Mind

Garage door openers get a workout; don't buy the cheapest model. A sturdy, middle-of-the-line model will last a very long time.

Building Porches and Decks

Porches and their roofless cousins—decks—are much less expensive to build than interior spaces, and dramatically extend your home's function and comfort. As a place to cook, socialize, or just watch the world go by, a well-designed and built porch or deck will repay its cost many times over.

Footings and Support System

Although they do not carry the weight of fully enclosed living spaces, porches and decks need firm foundations. Most often this is accomplished with concrete footings (set below the frost line) attached by rebar to concrete columns. These columns are often made with a columnar concrete form, made of cardboard, into which rebar is inserted for increased strength, and concrete is poured. The deck or porch floor is then built above these.

Porch and deck floors are built with a very slight pitch—about an inch for every 10 to 12 feet of floor run—*away* from the side of the house, so that water doesn't pool on the surface and begin to rot the wood of the floor, support system, or side of the house.

The Porch Roof

Porch roofs are often shallower than the house roof; this differentiates the space. And the porch roof can be made of a different material than the house roof. Metal—standing seamed tin or copper—looks great, weathers beautifully, lasts almost forever, and is an appropriate (though expensive) choice for a traditionally styled house. But there's no rule for the porch roof, except that a good-sized overhang will keep water away from its underlying support structure, ensuring that it will hold up longer against the elements.

Railings and Finishes

If the porch or deck floor is more than a certain number of inches above grade, it will need to be equipped with a railing.

The rules for railing a porch or deck depend on local code, but if you have children or grandchildren you'll want this security, no matter the legal requirements. And just as there are rules about the distance between balusters—the upright posts that support the handrail—on an interior staircase, there are rules about the balusters of a deck or porch railing. Usually, the space between upright supports must not allow a 6-inch sphere (roughly the size of an infant's head) to pass through it.

If you are going to use appliances, extra lighting, or other electrical equipment on your porch or deck, be sure to have sufficient receptacles installed. These must be weather-proof, with a cover over the plug to keep water out when they are not in use.

Outdoor Structures Worksheets

Indicate work done and materials used on the following pages.

Outdoor Structures Worksheet

Work/Materials Description	Start/Complete (Estimated)	Sub or Contact (Name or Company)
GARAGES		
Foundation		
☐ Labor		
☐ Materials		
Frame		
☐ Labor		
☐ Materials		
Roof		
☐ Labor		
☐ Materials		
Plumbing		
☐ Labor		
☐ Materials		
Electrical		
☐ Labor		
☐ Materials		
Other: _____		
☐ Labor		
☐ Materials		
Other: _____		
☐ Labor		
☐ Materials		
PORCHES		
Foundation		
☐ Labor		
☐ Materials		
Frame		
☐ Labor		
☐ Materials		

	Start Date	Cost (Estimated)	Cost (Actual)	Complete Date	Ck. #	Lien Waiver

Outdoor Structures Worksheet

Work/Materials Description	Start/Complete (Estimated)	Sub or Contact (Name or Company)
Roof		
☐ Labor		
☐ Materials		
Electrical		
☐ Labor		
☐ Materials		
Other: _____		
☐ Labor		
☐ Materials		
Other: _____		
☐ Labor		
☐ Materials		
DECKS		
Foundation		
☐ Labor		
☐ Materials		
Frame		
☐ Labor		
☐ Materials		
Electrical		
☐ Labor		
☐ Materials		
Other: _____		
☐ Labor		
☐ Materials		
Other: _____		
☐ Labor		
☐ Materials		

	Start Date	Cost (Estimated)	Cost (Actual)	Complete Date	Ck. #	Lien Waiver

Notes

Finish Work: Inside and Out

15

The term *finish work* is a bit misleading. It sounds as though you're almost done, but because finishes provide all the detailing in your house, the process is quite complex. Finishing the interior will take longer than framing it did.

Sweating the fine points of interior openings and hardware, cabinets, trim, fixtures, flooring, and countertops means that you'll be doing another round with your tradespeople—those who installed the rough-ins—plus a new group. Unless your carpenters are installing the cabinets, the kitchen company will send their crew, for cabinets and countertop and any special trims. Then there are the flooring subs, the tile installers, and so forth. Then there's the outside: your landscape and its main points, at least.

This large cast means that sometimes the perfect sequence won't happen. With the end in sight, it's hard not to hurry everyone along, but take care to let everyone do his best work.

You will have to protect existing finish work from other subs who might ding your freshly painted walls or scratch the new hardwood floors. Nothing is more frustrating than having to redo good work.

Be patient, hold your temper, and be prepared to spend a lot of time at the site.

Keep in Mind

Because finish sequences may vary, read through this entire section before your own finish work starts. You need to be aware of everything that gets done in this phase.

Interior Finish Checklist

Because the scope of your project and sequence of events may vary, make sure all items in your program get checked; enter N/A for those tasks that do not apply to your house.

Work for This Phase	Contact
☐ Prime ceilings and walls	_____
☐ Hardwood floor installation	_____
☐ Install underlayments tile and vinyl flooring	_____
☐ Cabinet installation	_____
☐ Install interior doors	_____
☐ Finish stairs	_____
☐ Install trim and baseboard	_____
☐ Interior paint	_____
☐ Install countertops	_____
☐ Install cabinet and door hardware	_____
☐ Install vinyl and tile floors; wall tile	_____
☐ HVAC trim	_____
☐ Plumbing trim	_____
☐ Electrical trim	_____
☐ Specialized trims	_____
☐ Phone	_____
☐ Intercom	_____
☐ Security	_____
☐ Audio/visual	_____
☐ Central vac	_____
☐ Other: _____	_____
☐ Other: _____	_____
☐ Install appliances	_____
☐ Accessory installation	_____
☐ Punch list (see Section 16)	_____
☐ Install carpet	_____
☐ Sand and finish hardwood floors	_____
☐ Touch-up paint	_____
☐ Clean-up	_____

Interior Prime Coat

After all the walls are hung and taped, and you've vacuumed and dusted throughout the house (the last step in Section 13), the painters can apply a coat of primer on walls and ceilings. Good preparation and priming will pave the way for a great-looking finish coat of paint or wallpaper.

Painting crews vary on the timing of the various coating applications for new walls and woodwork. Some painting subs may apply the ceiling paint at this time. It will then be ready for the electrical finish, when all the ceiling fixtures and trim are installed.

Flooring Installation

Hardwood floors and underlayments for tile and vinyl flooring come next. To protect the newly installed (but still unfinished) hardwood flooring, tape a layer of rosin paper to the base of the adjoining walls. Using plastic to cover a wood floor can trap moisture underneath and damage the flooring.

Kitchen floors are often installed only to the cabinet edges; this is not a problem when you move in. But later, if you or a future owner wants to remodel the kitchen, the floor will have to be redone.

Keep in Mind

If the dishwasher is installed on a finish floor rather than on the subflooring, this will affect its height (and that of any other under-counter appliance installations) relative to the planned countertop. Be sure there is sufficient clearance so that that dishwasher will open freely and the countertop height is not affected.

Transitions between flooring are best made under doors. Be sure that adjustments are made for material of varying heights so that these transitions do not become tripping hazards.

Cabinet Installation

Kitchen, bath, and other cabinets and built-ins can be installed or built onsite. Care and precision are the domain of the finish carpenter, so this work will be painstaking and may seem slow, particularly if you're having custom cabinetry installed.

Interior Door Installations

Even an open plan house—one with few partitions in the public areas—has interior doors for private spaces, bathrooms, and closets. Careful attention to the plans and specs will ensure that every door is installed properly in the correct location.

First, carefully inspect your delivery to see that your doors are of the correct material, size, and swing, and equipped with the proper hardware. You may want to label each one with its location on a piece of masking tape. This will help your subs set them up in the right order for installation.

Many homeowners select prehung interior doors that are primed and ready for a finish coat of paint; some are also available in a limited choice of pre-applied finishes. This may save a bit on your finish painting costs, because doors are labor-intensive to paint by hand.

Stairs

Stairs are complicated, so some owner-builders hire a stair company for this important step. Others leave the job to their finish carpenters; any experienced carpenter has built many stair runs.

Unless it's a simple, closed stair (one with walls on both sides and a handrail), a formal staircase requires many parts to create a safe, sturdy, and aesthetically pleasing passage between floors. The formal stair is often the centerpiece of your home's front entry, so you want the details right. This is another point for a walk-through—or at least a talk-through—of your vision with your subs.

Trim and Baseboard

Trim around windows and door openings, between the floors and walls (called base-boards, or in northern New England, *mopboards*), and between walls and ceilings (moldings), is like the collar and cuffs of a shirt. These finishes can be simple and straightforward, or dressy and complicated.

But no matter whether you choose a very plain trim pattern—clamshell and Colonial are the simplest types—or elaborate trims and moldings composed of several pieces, your subs should take care with the installation and the corners where pieces join. When the joints are caulked and the trim painted, the trims should look smooth, and the corners sharp and neat.

Interior Paint

Before finish work begins, you may want to have a discussion with your painting/wallpaper contractor about timing and whether his crew will do everything at once—prime, paint, and paper—or come at different stages of the finish (priming first, before any of the other finishes; then all other coatings and wallpaper, then a final touch-up when all finishes are complete). This is an individual choice between you and your subs, and it depends on your budget and time allotted for the work. Doing the job at three different times adds to set-up and clean-up labor, but may be worth it in the long run.

After the trim is installed, you are at a logical point for finish painting or wallpapering the interior walls. Whatever scope and sequence you decide on, timing is everything. Keep the painting/wallpaper subs informed if there are any delays; you'll have a better chance of keeping the desired sequence.

If you plan to stain woodwork, you may want this done just before your hardwood floors are finished. Check on the timing with your sub.

If your cabinetry is still being worked on, or all the trim is not yet installed, you may have to delay the paint or wallpaper. Keep these subs informed of the state of construction, so they can put you back on their schedules for later.

Countertops

Depending on how many countertops you have, what size they are, and where they are located, this step may come before or after this point. If your only countertop is in the kitchen, your kitchen installers may have already finished this step.

What you don't want to see are visible seams in your counters (unless seams—in a contrast material, for example—are part of the aesthetic of the countertop). Installation should be careful and precise. Because finish plumbing (sinks, faucets, and other fittings) will go in after the counters are installed, you want to be sure that the counters are correct before the plumbers move in.

Cabinet and Door Hardware

Once the interiors have been painted, the cabinet and door hardware can go on. If you are waiting for the finish coat on trim and openings, you can install hardware, but you will have to have the painters remove it or mask the metal finishes before they paint.

Tile Work, Vinyl, and Other Non-Wood Flooring

To install toilets, pedestal lavatories, and other floor-mounted fixtures and equipment, the finish floors must be in place. Enter your tile subcontractors, as well as the subs installing your vinyl, linoleum, and other non-wood floors.

The tile installers can also complete any tile walls, shower or tub surrounds, or other specialty tile work.

HVAC, Plumbing, Electrical, and Other Mechanical Finishes, Including Appliances

The pipes and wires have long been in the walls; now it's time to hook everything up. Receptacles and switches get their final control mechanisms and cover plates. Light fixtures, sconces, and chandeliers are hung and connected to the roughed-in wiring already in place. Pipes get attached to faucets and sinks. Thermostats connect to the heating/cooling source. Fans and vents become operable. And any other devices, from a central vacuum cleaner system to the security alarm and smoke and carbon monoxide detectors, get installed in their selected locations (many determined by your building codes).

If the timing is right, the tradespeople can also complete the exterior finishes now.

Check out each installation before the tradesperson leaves. Make sure you have the following information:

- How each system operates.
- How to shut down/restart each system and the emergency contact information for each system.
- A copy of the applicable warranty for each system and an understanding of its duration and degree of coverage (parts and labor, parts only, and so forth).

Keep in Mind

If your home is not connected to gas lines with a meter, and you are installing propane for a stove or backup heating system, be sure to follow local installation and inspection requirements. Most gas lines need to be checked and passed by an inspector before an appliance or furnace is hooked up.

Accessory Installation

Miscellaneous items find their places. Some examples:

- Closet poles and hooks
- Wire shelving
- Towel bars
- Toilet paper roll holders

This is the point where blocking—those pieces of 2-by-4s you had the carpenters install between studs during framing—comes in handy to anchor the little conveniences.

The Punch List

Now it's time for a top-to-bottom inspection of your home for anything left undone because of delivery delays, missing parts, or just because you or your subs missed a spot. Use the notes pages at the end of Section 16 to create a list. Date it when you make it, and as each item is completed, check it off, then initial and date it.

Although only a few finishing details remain, try not to chomp too much at the bit, and follow some owner-builder advice:

"It's tempting to move into your house before everything is done, but don't do it," says owner-builder Patti Garbeck. "Because I'm a carpenter by trade, I figured I could leave a few things undone and get to them after I moved in. Ten years later, I was still finishing the details. Avoid this trap, and *don't move in until the house is finished*." Owner-builder Siobhan Daggett-Terenzi moved into her finished basement while work on the main floor was going on, but despite the discomfort of living amid boxes, she and husband John did not move upstairs until the whole house was completed and in true move-in condition. Obviously, very strict building departments will not look kindly on a premature move-in. Regardless of local ordinances, however, most professional builders and owner-builders will advise you to spend a few weeks in a sympathetic friend's or relative's guest room rather than moving into an unfinished house.

Carpet Installation and Floor Finish

After everything else is done, the carpet installers can bring in their padding and yardage. You can add a shoe molding (a small quarter-round piece) to the baseboard moldings in carpeted rooms to give the joint where baseboard meets carpet a finished appearance. This addition will also conceal any nicks in the bottom edge of the baseboard from the carpet installers' equipment.

Now is also the time for the hardwood floor finishes to be applied, to dry, and to be followed by one or more protective layers of polyurethane (or wax, for the traditionalists).

While the floor is drying inside, the outside crew can finish the landscape details.

Exterior Finish Checklist

Be sure to check off each step as it is completed.

Work for This Phase	Contact
☐ Final grading	_____
☐ Exterior paint/stain	_____
☐ Install gutters	_____

Landscape (Hard Features)

☐ Walls	_____
☐ Fencing	_____

Other hard features (list):

☐ _____	_____
☐ _____	_____
☐ _____	_____
☐ _____	_____
☐ Electrical finishes	_____
☐ Plumbing finishes	_____
☐ Garden beds	_____
☐ Trees/shrubs installed	_____
☐ Grass seed	_____
☐ Exterior punch list (see Section 16)	_____
☐ Driveway and parking area paving	_____
☐ Mailbox	_____

Final Grading

Now is the time to call back your excavator to do the final grading for your property. You need to make sure that the ground slopes *away* from the house, alleviating water pressure on the foundation. You can also use the topsoil you set aside when the initial site work was done.

Exterior Paint and Stain

Because staining and sealing your siding is much less labor intensive than priming and painting, you may opt for this finish. Keep in mind, though, that stain must be reapplied and resealed at regular intervals, or the coating won't resist the weather. Stain and sealer require more frequent recoating than primer and paint.

Gutters

Gutters and downspouts are additional insurance against water damage to your house. Take care with the direction of water flow from downspouts. You don't want to take water from your roof and run it back toward the house.

Landscape Hard Features

Things such as walls, fences, and patio areas can go in after the property is graded, the paint work finished, and the gutters installed.

Keep in Mind

Patios adjacent to the walls of the house (next to sliders, or a screened porch, for example), should also slope slightly away from the house, or have drainage constructed so that they don't trap water against the foundation after heavy rains.

Electrical Finishes

Outdoor lighting and other outside features (weatherproof receptacles for electronics, for example) can be installed at this point. One receptacle on each side of the house is helpful. The garage door opener and other garage switches and receptacles can also go in now.

Don't forget lighting next to all the entrances, as well as any other spots.

Plumbing Finishes

Don't forget hose bibs on both sides of the house, to make dragging the garden hose around less of a chore. You may also want to install a hose reel at or near the bib for easy storage.

Installing Trees, Shrubs, and Plant Material

This is when your exterior will start to take on its finished appearance, even if the plants, shrubs, and trees are small.

If your area is populated by deer, net your tender new plantings so they don't become Bambi's dinner! Even better, invest in plants and shrubs that deer don't like. Your landscape architect or contractor will have some ideas; a good local nursery and your state's cooperative extension department are also good sources for advice on deer-resistant landscaping.

Pro Know-How

A good arborist—tree specialist in layman's language—will tell you that one of the mistakes owners make is planting small trees and shrubs too close together. They *will* grow, and when they do, crowding can kill expensive plantings, including much of an evergreen border. Remember to fence off the base of small deciduous trees to the circumference of each one's crown, and give evergreens room to expand without blocking each other's sun.

Grass Seed

You or your landscape crew can spread grass seed and straw over your lawn area. Keep the seed watered until it not only sprouts, but fills in. Otherwise you'll need to reseed in the next growing season.

Exterior Punch List

Take a careful walk around your property, looking for anything that has been left undone. Create your exterior punch list at the end of Section 16, with your interior punch list. Again, date the list, then check off and date each item as it is completed.

Paving Driveway and Parking Area

An asphalt-paved driveway, gravel pathway, or merely a cleared right-of-way may be the appropriate route for getting your car to your house. In any event, the final clearing and paving should wait for last, especially with asphalt. Heavy trucks can damage a new paving job.

When the driveway's done, your finishing touch will be a new mailbox!

Keep in Mind

If you've weathered all the storms of construction, you are probably in a celebratory mood. When you've finally moved in, you may want to have a little party for the subs who helped you get there. It doesn't have to be exotic or expensive: some snacks and a choice of beverages is nice. Your crew will appreciate seeing the house finished, and you'll have a chance to express your appreciation. It's a good way to end a very big project.

The Real Finish Checklist

Keep the following contact list handy, and check off each step when it's done.

Work for This Phase	Contact
Final inspections (list):	
☐ _____	_____
☐ _____	_____
☐ _____	_____
☐ _____	_____
☐ Bank inspection	_____
☐ Certificate of Occupancy	_____
☐ Cleanup	_____
☐ Mortgage closing or conversion of construction loan to mortgage	_____
☐ Final payments to subs	_____
☐ MOVING DAY!	_____

Finishing Up, for Real

During the rough-ins, and then through the excruciating detail of finish work, you may not have believed this phase of your project would ever come. But now it's here.

You're about to invite the inspector(s) for their final looks around. Your bank inspector will survey everything as well, to make sure work has been completed for your final draw. You'll be paying off subs, cleaning up your new house, and then awaiting the movers. It's an exciting time.

Enjoy your new home!

Finish Work Worksheets

Indicate work completed and materials used on the following pages.

Finish Work Worksheets

Work/Materials Description	Start/Complete (Estimated)	Sub or Contact (Name or Company)
INTERIOR FINISH		
Painting/Wallpaper		
☐ Prime coat (labor)		
☐ Finish coats (labor)		
☐ Wallpaper		
Painting/Wallpaper Materials:		
☐		
☐		
☐		
☐		
Hardwood Floors		
☐ Install labor		
☐ Install materials		
☐ Finish labor		
☐ Finish materials		
Other Flooring (list):		
☐		
☐ Labor install		
☐		
☐ Labor install		
☐		
☐ Labor install		
☐		
☐ Labor install		
Cabinet Installation		
☐ Kitchen		
☐ Labor install		
☐ Bath		
☐ Labor install		

	Start Date	Cost (Estimated)	Cost (Actual)	Complete Date	Ck. #	Lien Waiver

Finish Work Worksheets

Work/Materials Description	Start/Complete (Estimated)	Sub or Contact (Name or Company)
☐ Other:		
☐ Labor install		
Interior Doors		
☐ Materials		
☐ Labor		
Stairs		
☐ Materials		
☐ Labor		
Trim and Baseboard		
☐ Materials		
☐ Labor		
Countertop		
☐ Materials		
☐ Labor		
Hardware: Door and Cabinet		
☐ Materials		
☐ Labor		
HVAC Finish		
☐ Materials		
☐ Labor		
Plumbing Finish		
☐ Materials		
☐ Labor		
Electrical Finish		
☐ Materials		
☐ Labor		
Other Mechanicals (list):		
☐		
☐		

	Start Date	Cost (Estimated)	Cost (Actual)	Complete Date	Ck. #	Lien Waiver

Finish Work Worksheets

Work/Materials Description	Start/Complete (Estimated)	Sub or Contact (Name or Company)
☐		
☐		
☐		
Appliances		
☐ Equipment		
☐ Install		
Accessories		
☐ Materials		
☐ Install		
☐ Interior cleanup		
EXTERIOR FINISH		
Final Grading		
☐ Labor		
☐ Materials		
Exterior Paint/Stain		
☐ Labor		
☐ Materials		
Gutters and Downspouts		
☐ Labor		
☐ Materials		
Landscape (Hard Features)		
☐ Walls		
☐ Fencing		
☐ Other:		
☐ Other:		
Electrical Finishes		
☐ Labor		
☐ Materials		
☐ Plumbing finishes		

Start Date	Cost (Estimated)	Cost (Actual)	Complete Date	Ck. #	Lien Waiver

Finish Work Worksheets

Work/Materials Description	Start/Complete (Estimated)	Sub or Contact (Name or Company)
☐ Labor		
☐ Materials		
☐ Trees, shrubs, plants		
☐ Materials		
☐ Labor		
☐ Driveway, parking pave		
☐ Materials		
☐ Labor		
☐ Mailbox		
FINAL FINISH		
☐ Inspections		
☐ Bank inspection		
☐ Certificate of Occupancy		
☐ Mortgage closing		
☐ Moving		

	Start Date	Cost (Estimated)	Cost (Actual)	Complete Date	Ck. #	Lien Waiver

Notes

Master Tracker for Schedule and Budget

16

This section provides you with space to put the sequence of your whole project in order, and keep track of timing and budget concerns.

How to Use the Worksheets

Starting with Pre-building, list the elements of construction that pertain to your project in the sequence in which you carry them out. There are seven worksheets covering the construction phases from Sections 9 through 15. Each worksheet lets you enter the following information:

- **Description** Describe the step in the process; e.g., temporary phone service or property survey.
- **M** Is this an entry for Materials? If it is, check this box.
- **L** Is this an entry for Labor performed? If it is, check this box.
- **Contact** Enter the name of the contact for this entry, from your Contact Lists.
- **Estimate** Your preliminary cost estimate.
- **Actual** What you actually spend.
- **Start/Rec'd.** Enter the date the work starts or the material is delivered.
- **Complete** Enter the date the work is completed.
- **Paid** Enter the date on which the work is paid.
- **Ck. #** Enter the check(s) number(s).
- **Amount** Actual cost of work.
- **Lien Waiver** Indicate that you've received a waiver from a sub by entering the date it is signed and returned to you.

Update this information daily as you visit the site, receive deliveries, and talk with subs.

You may find it helpful to create a similar document on a computer spreadsheet that automatically calculates your costs and is easily correctable as numbers change with the flow of the project.

Pre-Building

Description	M	L	Contact	Estimate	Actual

	Start/Rec'd	Complete	Paid	Ck. #	Amount	Lien Waiver

Clearing, Excavation, Foundation

Description	M	L	Contact	Estimate	Actual

Start/Rec'd	Complete	Paid	Ck. #	Amount	Lien Waiver

Framing and Sheathing

Description	M	L	Contact	Estimate	Actual

	Start/Rec'd	Complete	Paid	Ck. #	Amount	Lien Waiver

Windows, Doors, and Siding

Description	M	L	Contact	Estimate	Actual

	Start/Rec'd	Complete	Paid	Ck. #	Amount	Lien Waiver

Rough-In, Closing Interior Walls

Description	M	L	Contact	Estimate	Actual

Start/Rec'd	Complete	Paid	Ck. #	Amount	Lien Waiver

Outside Structures: Porches, Garages, and Decks

Description	M	L	Contact	Estimate	Actual

	Start/Rec'd	Complete	Paid	Ck. #	Amount	Lien Waiver

Finish Work: Inside and Out

Description	M	L	Contact	Estimate	Actual

	Start/Rec'd	Complete	Paid	Ck. #	Amount	Lien Waiver

Punch Lists

When you walk through the project as the various subcontractors finish their work, make note of anything that still needs to be done or corrected. The subs may fix it immediately, or come back at the end. It's ideal to get things done right away, although small details like paint touch-ups can take place at the last opportunity before move-in. Cross off each task that you list when it's complete.

Interior

_____

_____

_____

_____

_____

_____

_____

_____

_____

_____

_____

_____

_____

_____

_____

_____

_____

_____

_____

_____

_____

_____

_____

_____

_____

_____

Exterior

_____
_____
_____
_____
_____
_____
_____
_____
_____
_____
_____
_____
_____
_____
_____
_____
_____
_____
_____
_____
_____
_____
_____
_____
_____
_____
_____
_____
_____
_____
_____
_____

Owner-Builder Dictionary

amps (amperes)   A unit of measurement for the speed of electron flow in electric current.

assembly   A set of components before they're put together.

benchmark   A sign or stake, set on the lot by a surveyor to show the exact height of the top of a building foundation. It is usually offset—placed away from the excavation site—so that it is not disturbed by earth-moving equipment.

bleeding   Removing the air from a hot water heating system by releasing air from individual radiator valves. This provides consistent heat throughout the system.

boiler   The heating plant for systems that heat and move water or steam through pipes.

caulk   A material used to create a watertight seal between two adjoining surfaces.

change order   In contracted construction or renovation, a written document authorizing a change in the scope, detail, characteristics, and/or cost of work specified in the contract. This document is signed and dated by the parties named in the contract.

chase   A channel in the wall of a structure that holds vents, pipes, and/or wires, providing space for them to run from room to room or floor to floor.

circuit   A loop through which electrical current can flow, beginning and ending at the same point. Household electrical circuits begin and end at the electrical panel, which receives its current from electric utility service lines that enter at the top of the panel.

circuit breaker   A device that stops the flow of electricity in a circuit if there is too much current for safe operation. Both toggle switches and fuses act as circuit breakers, but only the toggle-switch type are commonly referred to as circuit breakers.

clerestory   The upper part of a wall. Window openings along this upper part of the wall are known as *clerestory windows.*

conductor   A medium that allows heat, electricity, light, or sound to pass through or along it. Copper wire is a good conductor of electrical current.

curb cut   Driveway egress from a property to the adjacent road.

CWF   Abbreviation for clear wood finish, used on exterior siding or interior woodwork to reveal the natural wood graining.

detail   In construction drawings, close-ups of complex structural elements.

drywall   The most common type of base wall material. It is made by sandwiching a gypsum core, which is fire resistant, between layers of paper. Also known as Sheetrock, wallboard, or gypsum board, this material is also made in a water-resistant variety for use in damp areas.

DWV   Abbreviation for drain, waste, and vent, commonly used in plumbing pipe descriptions.

electricity   The flow of electrons through a conductor.

elevation   In a set of construction drawings, two-dimensional drawings of each side of a building.

fenestration   The architectural term for the design and placement of windows in a building.

furnace   The heating plant for forced-air systems—the majority of systems in the United States—that heat air and then move it, by means of a blower, through a system of ducts.

furring strips   Thin, narrow pieces of wood used to provide backing to support a finished surface.

gasket   A material that creates a seal between two surfaces—for example, a door and its opening.

gauge   The sizing system for the diameter of wire. The smaller the gauge number, the larger the diameter of the wire.

grade   The level at which the ground meets a structure.

ground fault circuit interrupter (GFCI)   A device used in code-compliant electrical receptacles near water sources. The GFCI almost instantly cuts power to a circuit if it detects a leakage of electric current.

GWB   Abbreviation for gypsum wallboard. (*See also* drywall.)

header   The horizontal part of a door or window frame.

ionizing filter   An air-cleaning device that gives tiny particles a charge that makes them stick to the surface of the filter until they are cleaned off.

jamb   The vertical part of the frame of an opening, either a window or a door.

joint   In carpentry, the intersection of two pieces of wood. There are many different kinds of wood joints.

joist   The framing that supports a floor or ceiling.

kilowatt hour (kWh)   A unit of energy equivalent to one kilowatt (1 kW) of power used for one hour (1 h).

lath   Used as the foundation for plaster or sometimes for tile. It is traditionally a framework of thin wood strips, or, more recently, wire mesh.

lien waiver   A document signed by a contractor or subcontractor certifying that payment for a contracted service or material for a property has been received. This document prevents the signer from later making a legal claim on the property in question.

lumber, dimensional   Lumber that is cut and finished to standardized width and depth specified in inches.

LVL   Abbreviation for laminated veneer lumber, often used for engineered trusses and other structural house parts.

mastic   A flexible cement used as an adhesive for affixing tile to an underlying surface.

MDF   Abbreviation for medium-density fiberboard, an engineered wood product formed under pressure from wood pulp ground to a powder, wax, and resin. It is often used for the unseen and unfinished surfaces of built-in kitchen cabinetry. Painted or stained, it is also used for some types of paneling.

mortar   The material used to fill gaps between blocks in masonry construction.

mortise   A hole or slot cut into wood or other material so that a projecting piece (called a *tenon*) can be precisely inserted. Mortise-and-tenon joints are a very sturdy joinery technique used in woodworking and carpentry.

OSB   Abbreviation for oriented strand board, sometimes called waferboard, which is a type of engineered wood composed of layered strips of wood, compressed and bonded together with wax and adhesive. OSB is similar to plywood, but in many applications is stronger and cheaper to use.

PEX   Cross-linked polyethylene tubing, used for residential water supply piping and hydronic radiant floor heating.

plan   In construction drawings, an overhead view of the layout of various levels of a structure, traditionally showing all elements visible at 5 feet above the floor. For residences, a set of construction documents will usually include plans for the foundation, living levels, and often, the roof.

pneumatic   Refers to a tool or machine that is operated by compressed air.

program   Architectural language for a list of the spaces, and the desired characteristics of those spaces, that will be translated into working drawings, then constructed as a building and its surroundings.

PVC   Polyvinyl chloride, used to make a variety of piping, especially waste lines.

rafters   The sloping, supporting timbers or boards that run from the ridge to the edge of the roof.

rails   The horizontal framing pieces of a window sash or door.

rebar   Common steel reinforcing bar, used as a component of reinforced concrete.

ridge   The long, straight center timber at the joint between the sloping sides of a gabled roof.

rough openings   Parts of the house frame that will be filled by windows, doors, skylights, chimneys, ducting and wiring, and stairways.

sash   The part of a window that holds one or more panes of glass or other transparent or translucent material.

schedule   A chart or table in a set of construction drawings that details materials, equipment, or finishes for a project.

section   An architectural drawing that shows a view of a vertical cut through a structure.

septic system   A small-scale sewage treatment system, used mainly in areas where there is no available municipal sewer system. Private septic systems usually consist of a holding tank and adjacent leaching field.

setback   The distance, required by law, between a property line and a building or other structure on the property.

shim   A thin, wedge-shaped piece of wood, metal, plastic, or cardboard. It's used to help position something properly by filling a gap, or to protect a surface from something that may scratch or mar it.

sidelight   A window positioned next to a door.

slab   Term for a flat concrete foundation, usually strengthened with rebar.

solvent   A substance in which other substances are dissolved.

spirit level   An instrument designed to indicate whether a surface is level (horizontal measure) or plumb (measured vertically).

square   Measurement used for roofing and shingle siding; a square is equivalent to 100 square feet.

stiles   The vertical framing pieces of a window sash or door.

supply stops   On/off controls found along household utility supply lines, managing the flow of gas or water to individual fixtures and appliances.

survey   A detailed map showing the area and dimensions of a piece of property, indicating its boundaries and significant features. A *topographical* survey also shows elevations.

take-off   A list of materials and supplies needed to build a house.

tempered glass   Glass that has been heated and cooled repeatedly in a controlled environment to give it more strength than conventional, single-layer window glass. Tempered glass is often required by code when used in entry doors.

timber   Lumber that is thicker than the nominal 5 inches.

topography   The features on the surface of a piece of land.

volt   A measure of the force with which electrons move in electrical current.

watt   A measure of electrical output.

Owner-Builder Resources

B

When you're building a house, you've got plenty to learn. Luckily, there's no shortage of information.

Helpful Organizations

The following professional and trade organizations offer helpful information and great ideas and tips. Many organization websites provide searchable lists to help you locate member professionals in your area.

The American Institute of Architects (AIA)   www.aia.org

American Lighting Association (ALA)   www.americanlightingassoc.com

American Society of Interior Designers (ASID)   www.asid.org

American Society of Landscape Architects (ASLA)   www.asla.org

Canadian Home Builders' Association   www.chba.ca

Custom Electronic Design & Installation Association (CEDIA)   www.cedia.net

Hearth, Patio & Barbecue Association (HPBA)   www.hpba.org

Insulation Contractors Association of America (ICAA)   www.insulate.org

National Association of Home Builders (NAHB)   www.nahb.org

National Burglar & Fire Alarm Association (NBFAA)   www.alarm.org

Painting and Decorating Contractors of America (PDCA)   www.pdca.org

Plumbing-Heating-Cooling Contractors Association (PHCC)   www.phccweb.org

Hands-On Education

One way to experience homebuilding in action is to volunteer with an organization involved in home construction. Habitat for Humanity is one, and there are a number of others. A few weekends of toting lumber, nailing up siding, and hanging sheetrock will provide you with newfound empathy for your subs and the jobs they will do for you. You'll also be better able to evaluate quality work.

Or take an education vacation before you build. Several schools and homebuilding institutes cater to owner-builders who want to contract their own homes. Most of these courses are given during a weekend; some extend for two or three weeks. Write for catalogs or research online:

Heartwood School for the Homebuilding Crafts, Washington, MA
www.heartwoodschool.com

Shelter Institute, Woolwich, ME   www.shelterinstitute.com

Southface Home Building School, Atlanta, GA   www.southface.org/web/
programs&events/courses&training/hbs/sf_homebuilding-school.htm

Yestermorrow Design/Build School, Warren, VT   www.yestermorrow.org

Your Owner-Builder Library

Here are some great books, as well as links to helpful articles to increase your know-how. An asterisk (*) indicates my favorites.

Part 1: Planning

Haun, Larry. *Habitat for Humanity: How to Build a House* (Taunton Press, 2002). With years of experience as a Habitat volunteer, and decades of work as a master builder, Larry Haun walks you through the entire construction process, start to finish, with lots of pictures. Although the illustrated project is a basic Habitat house, the sequencing and details are accurate and instructive.

Kidder, Tracy. *House* (Mariner Books, 1999). A national best-seller when it was first published in 1985, this narrative provides an intimate view of the dynamics among owner-builders, the architect, and the contractors as a dream house is conceived and then built. Says Home Team member Andrea Donnelly, "Anyone who builds a house should read this book."

Locke, Jim. *The Well-Built House* (Houghton Mifflin, 1992). Here's a contractor's-eye view of the custom house-building process. The author, a builder, shares dozens of important and informative details that only a pro would know. It gets you inside the mind of an experienced craftsman—just the sort of professional you want to hire for your project.

Green Building Information

Energy efficiency and sustainable materials and practices are now part of the new home equation. Everything from locating the house to structural design, materials, and systems choices will affect not only the cost to build the house, but the cost to use and maintain it.

Here are a few places to gather information:

Wilson, Alex. *Your Green Home* (New Society Publishers, 2006). Wilson has been involved with green and sustainable building for more than 30 years. This is a great introduction to all things green.

The U.S. Department of Energy's division of Energy Efficiency and Renewable Energy has a huge amount of information for home builders. Visit www.buildingamerica.gov for downloadable booklets for every area of the country (based on climate type). You'll find helpful information for every phase of your project, from locating the house on your lot to finish materials.

*After you have plans and specifications, you can give your project a do-it-yourself energy audit. Go to hes.lbl.gov, a site developed by the Environmental Energy Technologies Division at Lawrence Berkeley National Laboratory. There's a comprehensive FAQ about all things energy-related. To do the energy audit, enter the zip code of your new home, and enter all the information you have about it, starting with square footage, number of windows, and type of heating/cooling system. When you're done, you can get a prescription on how to improve the efficiency of your design.

Budget and Finance

Means Residential Cost Data for the current year (or a recent one), is a great reference tool for estimating home construction costs. Location factors for more than 900 U.S. zip codes and Canadian locations allow you to adjust costs. Although it's not inexpensive, you may find it worthwhile to have your own copy. It's also available in a CD-ROM version. Your architect or local library may also have a recent copy to lend. For more information, go to the company's website: www.rsmeans.com/bookstore/detail. asp?sku=60178.

Site

Scher, Les, and Carol Scher. *Finding & Buying Your Place in the Country* (Kaplan Business, 2000). Explores many of the issues involved in buying, owning, and building on country property. This volume is most valuable for the owner-builder who's doing construction on rural acreage.

Chalofsky, Barry. *The Home and Land Buyer's Guide to the Environment* (Rutgers University, 1997). Provides excellent advice for locating critical information about a property—from zoning to water issues. The author, a licensed professional planner, addresses dozens of land-related issues and directs the reader to the appropriate offices and agencies.

"Protecting Trees from Construction Damage: A Homeowner's Guide." A great article written for the University of Minnesota Cooperative Extension service. Find it on the web at www.extension.umn.edu/distribution/housingandclothing/DK6135.html.

For everything you want to know about installing wells and septic systems, check out the American Ground Water Trust: www.agwt.org/index.htm. Click "Ground Water Information" to download comprehensive files on installing water wells and septic systems and learn how they work.

Plans

Ready-made (stock) plans: There are hundreds of books of house plans. Here are a couple of sources I feel have particularly attractive plans:

Lucia's Little Houses   www.luciaslittlehouses.com

Architect Robert Knight designs captivating custom houses—from tiny cottages to waterside family compounds—for attractive vacation spots. With the owners' permission, Knight sells house plans of some of these designs to the general public. View them at this site; you can also order an inexpensive ($20) book of 20 small house plans via the website.

Arts and Crafts House Plans   www.thompsonplans.com

Architect Rick Thompson loaned some of his drawings and a materials list for this book. Thompson, whose bungalow-style houses are popular nationwide, is also developing a new website, at www.sustainablehouseplans.com, dedicated to plans that focus on green principles and energy efficiency.

Although Knight's plans are geared for more rural lots, many of Thompson's plans are ideal for narrow lots in well-developed areas.

Working with an Architect

Morosco, Gerald. *How to Work with an Architect* (Gibbs Smith, 2006). Written by an architect, this book has a discernible point of view. It also has helpful tips and information for getting the best results from collaboration with an architect or professional designer.

Modular Houses

The National Association of Home Builders (NAHB) has links to lists of modular builders, arranged by region. Access it at www.nahb.org/directory.aspx?sectionID=816&directoryID=340.

Author Sheri Koones has been reporting on custom modular homes for several years. Both of her books—*Modular Mansions* (Gibbs Smith, 2005) and *Prefabulous* (Taunton Press, 2007)—will help you understand the process and contain valuable information about companies currently manufacturing modular designs.

Materials

Koones, Sheri. *House About It* (Gibbs Smith, 2004). An encyclopedic volume of information about house styles and parts to help owner-builders choose among available materials. Plenty of sources, complete with phone numbers and websites.

Wilson, Alex. *Green Building Products.* (New Society, 2006). Another great "green" manual from Wilson, who knows his way around these products—as editor and publisher of the trade newsletter *Building Green,* he's been reviewing green materials for years. If you're intent on building a resource-conserving, energy-efficient house, this volume provides plenty of sources for good green stuff.

The Sweets comprehensive catalogs of almost any material you could want for a house or building, arranged by CSI specifications formats (see below), offer a quick way to browse the thousands of materials available. You can check with your library to see if there's a recent edition in the reference section. You can also ask to see or borrow your architect's copies. Or register and join the Sweets Network online. For information go to: products.construction.com/portal/server.pt.

Construction Specifications Institute (CSI MasterFormat)   To download a copy of the 2004—48 division—Edition, go to www.csinet.org/s_csi/sec.asp?TRACKID=&CID=13 77&DID=11339. Click the PDF download.

For a listing of the 16 divisions, 1995 version, go to www.constructionnotebook.com/ipin2/CSIDivisions.asp.

Lumber

This Old House magazine is worth the cost of a subscription; it's full of good information about materials, tools, and practices.

You want your framing crew to use the best possible lumber. Check out these articles from the magazine online to learn everything you need to know:

"The Language of Lumber"   www.thisoldhouse.com/toh/article/0,,1637858,00.html

"How to Read the Stamp"   www.thisoldhouse.com/toh/article/0,,1639800,00.html

Fasteners

Home improvement center Lowe's has lots of helpful guidance on its website. Link to a comprehensive chart: www.lowes.com/lowes/lkn?action=howTo&p=BuyGuide/ChsFastnrNailScrew.html&rn=RightNavFiles/rightNavHardware.

Hard-to-Find Materials

If you like vintage details and can't find the right antique or reproduction light fixtures, plumbing fixtures, faucets, doorknobs, and other period items, these companies' catalogs and websites can help:

Van Dyke's Restorers has all manner of wonderful reproduction house parts, from drawer pulls to claw foot bathtubs. Go to www.vandykes.com or call 1-800-787-3355 for a free catalog.

Here are some sources for Victorian, Art Deco, or mid-century modern lighting:

- **Rejuvenation:** Fixtures and hardware, Colonial Revival through Art Deco www.rejuvenation.com
- **Schoolhouse Electric:** Wonderful period reproductions www.schoolhouseelectric.com
- **Design Within Reach:** Mid-twentieth-century modern fixtures to complement design and furnishings with roots in the 1950s and '60s   www.dwr.com

Salvage: Using old house parts in new homes has gotten easier than ever. Most major cities now have at least one salvage operation that resells old moldings, mantels, cabinets, hardware, stone, brick, and wood planks. Check your local phone listings or try this wide-ranging web resource: www.oldhouseweb.com/links/pages/Architectural_Salvage.

Suppliers

Materials take-off: If you love numbers and figuring quantities and costs, you may want to do your own materials take-off, to compare it with your architect's and/or supplier's numbers.

DelPico, Wayne J. *Plan Reading & Material Takeoff* (Reed Construction Data, 1994). A fairly comprehensive volume that will help a DIY estimator take a crack at getting the numbers right.

Part 2: Construction

Fine Homebuilding, a magazine largely written by pros for pros, gets down to the nitty-gritty details of creating a custom house, inside and out. If you want a quick education, spend plenty of time immersed in this magazine's current and back issues. The publisher, Taunton Press (www.tauntonpress.com), sells annual back-issue compilations on DVD that make searching the archives easy.

Foundations

Concrete—the stuff of foundations—is best handled by expert foundation contractors. To learn more, visit the FAQ page of a concrete supplier in New Hampshire. You'll learn most of the basics: www.carrollconcrete.com/Page/Frequently-Asked-Questions-Products.

Frame

Pressure-treated lumber: For information about the new generation of less toxic, pressure-treated products, see this *Fine Homebuilding* piece on the subject: www.taunton.com/finehomebuilding/how-to/articles/new-pressure-treated-wood-decks.aspx.

Engineered wood trusses and beams: APA—The Engineered Wood Association has a lot of online information about engineered wood products. Investigate at www.apawood.org/level_b.cfm?content=prd_main.

Tables and Lists You Can Use

Dimensional Lumber Sizes

During the course of shopping for lumber and building your house, you'll hear short-hand phrases such as "One by," "Four by," or, even more mysterious, "Five four." Unless you've lived around lumberyards all your life, you may not know that these are *nominal* (name only) dimensions of softwood and hardwood lumber. The *actual* (true) dimensions will be somewhat smaller, due to the fact that lumber shrinks as it dries. Here are charts for dimensional lumber sizes for both soft- and hardwood.

Softwood

Standard lengths for softwood lumber are in increments of 2 feet; i.e., 6, 8, 10, 12, and so on up to 24 feet.

Nominal	Actual	Nominal	Actual
1×2	¾"×1 ½"	2×6	1 ½"×5 ½"
1×3	¾"×2 ½"	2×8	1 ½"×7 ¼"
1×4	¾"×3 ½"	2×10	1 ½"×9 ¼"
1×6	¾"×5 ½"	2×12	1 ½"×11 ¼"
1×8	¾"×7 ¼"	2×14	1 ½"×13 ¼"
1×10	¾"×9 ¼"	3×4	2 ½"×3 ½"
1×12	¾"×11 ⅝"	4×4	3 ½"×3 ½"
2×2	1 ½"×1 ½"	4×6	3 ½"×5 ½"
2×3	1 ½"×2 ½"	6×6	5 ½"×5 ½"
2×4	1 ½"×3 ½"	8×8	7 ¼"×7 ¼"

Hardwood

Hardwoods are sold by the board foot (12"×12"×1" [nominal] thick)

Thickness measurements use the *quarter* system with a nominally 1-inch-thick board called 4/4 (four quarter).

Nominal	S1S: Surfaced One Side	S2S: Surfaced Two Sides
½"	⅜"	⁵⁄₁₆"
⅝"	½"	⁷⁄₁₆"
¾"	⅝"	⁹⁄₁₆"
4/4 (1")	⅞"	¹³⁄₁₆"
5/4 (1 ¼")	1 ⅛"	1 ¹⁄₁₆"
6/4 (1 ½")	1 ⅜"	1 ⁵⁄₁₆"
8/4 (2")	1 ¹³⁄₁₆"	1 ¾"
12/4 (3")	2 ¹³⁄₁₆"	2 ¾"
16/4 (4")	3 ¹³⁄₁₆"	3 ¾"

The Rules About Tools

A good GC is ready to jump in and help when needed; you should be prepared with your own tools. Do not borrow them from your subs.

Mac Rood teaches owner-builders the fine points of home construction at the Yestermorrow Design/Build School in Vermont and suggests the following tools for the GC.

The set of tools a GC owns depends on the type of GC you are. A deskbound manager type might only require a tape measure in addition to an office computer. But you might also want a transit or builder's level and various other "layout" type tools. A carpenter/DIY/GC would definitely own power tools and a full complement of hand tools. Here's a basic list.

Hand tools in your nail apron/tool belt:

- Hammer (I think the straight claw version is most versatile)
- Tape measure
- Chalk line
- Bevel square
- Combination square or "speed square" (similar but different)
- Screwdriver with interchangeable tips
- Chisel
- Utility knife with retractable blade
- Nail set

- Pencil
- Safety glasses and ear protection

Other hand tools:

- Cat's paw
- Crow bar
- Wonder bar (a flat pry bar)
- One or more sizes of hand saws
- Sledgehammer (the persuader)
- 100" or 150" tape measure(s)
- Level

Minimum power tools:

- Circular saw
- Reversible 3/8" variable speed drill
- Jig saw
- Table saw

Desirable power tools:

- Pneumatic nailers (if you want to graduate from a hammer)
- Reciprocating saw (for rough or demolition work)
- Various sanders

Window Performance Measurements

The National Fenestration Rating Council (NFRC) certifies the performance of member manufacturers' products. You may see labels on your windows with an NFRC logo. Here is what the numbers mean:

- **U-Factor:** This is a measurement of how well a product prevents heat from escaping a home or building.

  Rating numbers: Generally between .20 and 1.20

  What they mean: The lower the number, the better the product for keeping heat in.

- **Solar Heat Gain Coefficient (SHGC):** This is a measurement of how well a product blocks heat from the sun.

Rating numbers: Between 0 and 1.

What they mean: The lower the SHGC, the better a product is at blocking heat gain.

■ **Visible Transmittance (VT):** This measures how much light comes through a product.

Rating numbers: Between 0 and 1.

What they mean: The higher the VT, the higher the potential for daylighting.

■ **Air Leakage (AL):** A measure of how much outside air penetrates into a building through the product.

Rating numbers: Between 0.1 and 0.3.

What they mean: The lower the AL, the better the product keeps air out. This is an optional rating and may not appear on the label.

■ **Condensation Resistance (CR):** This measures how well the product resists the formation of condensation.

Rating numbers: Between 1 and 100.

What they mean: The higher the number, the better the product resists condensation. This is an optional rating and may not appear on the label.

■ **Energy Star:** These labels on windows indicate excellent efficiency; the labels also carry a map that shows which part of the country is rated highly. For example, windows with a low SHGC number work well in hot climates; windows with a low U-factor hold in heat in colder parts of the country.

Architectural Plan Symbols

Many architects and stock plan sets will provide their own keys for reading the elements of construction drawings. Often, though, not all the symbols are referenced in the key. The following table gives you an overview.

Common Architectural Symbols

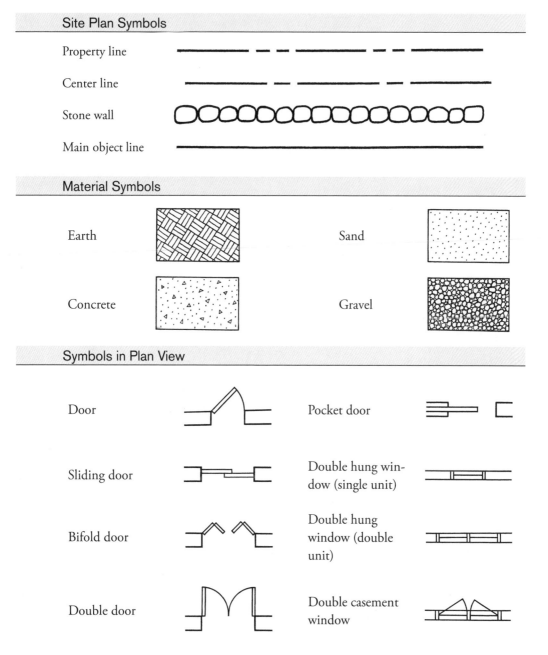

Site Plan Symbols	
Property line	
Center line	
Stone wall	
Main object line	

Material Symbols			
Earth		Sand	
Concrete		Gravel	

Symbols in Plan View			
Door		Pocket door	
Sliding door		Double hung window (single unit)	
Bifold door		Double hung window (double unit)	
Double door		Double casement window	

Fixtures in Plan View

Stove		Toilet	
Washer		Single sink vanity	
Dryer		Shower	
Bathtub		Kitchen sink	

Electrical Symbols *

Switch	$	Duplex floor receptacls	
Three-way switch	$₃	Smoke alarm	S
Duplex floor receptacle		Recessed lighting fixture	
Weatherproof duplex receptacle	WP		

Other Symbols

Electric door opener	D	Supply duct HVAC	
Thermostat	T	Return duct HVAC	

Dotted lines are often drawn between switches and the fixtures and/or receptacles they control. Symbol drawings by Karen Burgess.

Construction Abbreviations: A Master List

Designers tend to be individualists. When a drawing is done by hand, sometimes abbreviations are written in lowercase letters, sometimes in uppercase, sometimes in a combination. The abbreviations in CAD (computer-assisted design) drawings are generally written in all uppercase.

ADJ	adjustable		**DR**	door
AFF	above finished floor		**DWG**	drawing
ALUM	aluminum		**EXG**	existing
BD	board		**EXT**	exterior
BLK	block		**FD**	floor drain
BM	beam		**FJ**	floor joist
CIP	cast-in-place		**FTG**	footing
CJ	ceiling joist		**GA**	gauge
CLG	ceiling		**GALV**	galvanized
CLO	closet		**GL**	glass
CMU	concrete masonry unit		**GWB**	gypsum wall board
CO	cased opening		**HC**	hollow core
COL	column		**HVAC**	heating, ventilation, and air conditioning
CONC	concrete			
CONT	continuous		**INS**	insulation
CPT	carpet		**INT**	interior
CT	ceramic tile		**JST**	joist
CWF	clear wood finish		**LVL**	laminated veneer lumber
DBL	double		**MECH**	mechanical
DF	Douglas fir		**MIL**	.001 inch
DJ	double joist		**MIN**	minimum
DN	down		**MTL**	metal

NIC	not in contract		**SF**	square foot
NTS	not to scale		**SHW**	shower
OC	on center (sometimes, O/C)		**SPF**	spruce pine fir
OPNG	opening		**SYP**	southern yellow pine
OSB	oriented strand board		**T&B**	top and bottom
PC	pull cord, or pre-cast		**T&G**	tough and groove
PEX	cross-linked polyethylene tubing		**TOP**	top of plate
PT	pressure treated, or paint		**VIF**	verify in field
PTN	partition		**WD**	wood
PSF	pounds per square foot		**WDW**	window
R	riser		**WH**	water heater
R/A	return air		**WWM**	welded wire mesh
REQD	required		**W/**	with
RM	room		**YP**	yellow pine
RO	rough opening			

Sample Materials List

This materials list is courtesy of Rick Thompson, who creates such lists for a small fee for purchasers of his plans. It is a general list, not matched to the construction drawings in this book. Along with the list, he adds the following caveat, as each building site and modification will change the final list of materials.

"Rick Thompson, Architects, Inc. accepts no responsibility for the specific quantity or qualities of the materials listed. The builder of each house must review the drawings and material list and judge for himself the suitability of this house for your specific site and local codes. The material list reflects an exact computer take off of materials without adjusting for waste, dead wood, stairs, site specific issues, or temporary braces."

Crawl Foundation

Foundation/ Type	Description	Location	Quantity	Unit
Fdn/crawl	2×6 pt plate	8" block	136.568	LF
Fdn/crawl	Anchor bolts	8" block	27.314	Pieces
Fdn/crawl	Concrete block	8" block	417.017	Pieces
Fdn/crawl	Insulation, sill gasket	8" block	136.568	LF
Fdn/crawl	Mortar type N	8" block	7.414	CF
Fdn/crawl	Poured concrete	24" ftg	8.71	CY
Fdn/crawl	Rebar ½", #4 3 bars	24" ftg	423.718	LF
Fdn/crawl	Stucco over masonry wall	8" block	370.682	SF
Fdn/garage	4" washed gravel	4" slab	3.96	CY
Fdn/garage	6 mil. film	4" slab	288	SF
Fdn/garage	Concrete slab	4" slab	3.96	CY
Fdn/garage	Poured concrete	24" ftg	2.796	CY
Fdn/garage	Rebar ½", #4 3 bars	24" ftg	136	LF
Fdn/garage	Welded wire mesh	4" slab	288	SF
Fdn/porch	Poured concrete ftg	24" ftg	0.493	CY
Fdn/porch ftg	Rebar ½", #4 3 bars	24" ftg	24	LF

Framing, by Story

Location	Description	Quantity	Unit
Fdn/crawl grdr	2×10×16	10	Each
Framing clg	2×10×8	4	Each
Framing clg	2×12×12	2	Each
Framing clg	2×6×12	21	Each
Framing clg	2×8×10	6	Each
Framing clg	2×8×12	6	Each
Framing clg	2×8×16	36	Each
Framing fl1	2×10×10	16	Each
Framing fl1	2×10×12	9	Each
Framing fl1	2×10×14	13	Each

Location	Description	Quantity	Unit
Framing fl1	2×10×16	17	Each
Framing fl1	2×10×16 pt	3	Each
Framing fl1	2×10×8 pt	3	Each
Framing fl1	2×8×8 pt	9	Each
Framing fl2	2×10×10	4	Each
Framing fl2	2×10×12	9	Each
Framing fl2	2×10×14	13	Each
Framing fl2	2×10×16	41	Each
Framing fl2	2×10×16 pt	3	Each
Framing fl2	2×10×8 pt	3	Each
Framing fl2	2×12×12	3	Each
Framing fl2	2×8×8 pt	9	Each
Framing header	2×10×16	7	Each
Framing roof	2×6×2"	3	Each
Framing roof	2×6×4"	33	Each
Framing roof	2×6×6"	23	Each
Framing roof	2×6×8"	29	Each
Framing roof	2×6×10"	52	Each
Framing roof	2×6×12"	4	Each
Framing roof	2×6×14"	57	Each
Framing roof	2×10×4"	1	Each
Framing roof	2×10×6"	1	Each
Framing roof	2×10×8"	1	Each
Framing roof	2×10×10"	1	Each
Framing roof	2×10×12"	1	Each
Framing roof	2×10×14"	3	Each
Framing roof	2×10×16"	2	Each
Framing roof	2×10×26"	2	Each
Framing roof	2×10×42"	1	Each
Framing roof	LUMBER OVERALL	2200.67	BF
Porch steps	Porch steps, pt	1	Each
Stairs	Drywall mud	0.01	5 gal. pail
Stairs	Drywall tape	0.021	Roll
Stairs	GWB 4" × 8" × ½"	0.325	Sheet
Stairs	Subflooring, plywood T&G ¾" CDX	0.325	Sheet

General Materials

Description	Quantity	Unit
#30 Felt	19.422	Square
1×8 #2SPF	491.139	LF
2×4 plate x 3	1682.95	LF
2×4-10 Hem fir Wd Stud 16oc	68.705	Pieces
2×4-8 Hem fir Wd Stud 16oc	231.432	Pieces
2×4-9 Hem fir Wd Stud 16oc	245.765	Pieces
3" crown	214.962	LF

Description	Quantity	Unit
$3/8$" plywood soffit	8.561	Sheet
Asphalt shingle	19.422	Square
Base	492.628	LF
Base 2 sides	186.003	LF
Bldg permit, total job	1	Each
Bldg cleanup	1	Each
Cedar shingles	202.25	SF
Closet shelves, 12"	28.971	LF
Corner board 5/4×6	307.156	LF
Drywall mud	5.054	5 gal. pail
Drywall tape, 250" roll	10.108	Roll
Fiberglass insulation, floor R-	732.026	SF
Fiberglass insulation, wall R-	2246.96	SF
Fiberglass insulation, ceiling R-	712	SF
Gas connection	1	Each
Gutters, .032 aluminum	202.613	LF
GWB, 4"×8"×½"	186.85	Sheet
GWB, type X, 4"× 8"×½"	5.718	Sheet
Handrail	43.938	Feet
Lattice	21.947	Feet
Metal drip edge	276.177	LF
Paint—ext.	9.194	Gallon
Paint—ext. primer	9.194	Gallon
Paint—int.	19.283	Gallon
Paint—int. primer	19.283	Gallon
Pantry/linen shelves ×5	28.242	LF
Porch posts, 8×8	6	Each
Porch railing, pt	63.399	LF
PT deck surface, 5/4×6	560.854	LF
Rake mold	99.991	LF
Rectangular louver, 18×30	2	Each
Ridge vent, shingle covered	79.243	LF
Sewer connection, 4" PVC	1	Each
Sheathing ½"	137.238	Sheet
Siding	2282.58	SF
Site preparation	1	Each
Soffit vents, 3"	176.186	LF
Stock plans from architect	1	Each
Subflooring, plywood T&G ¾" CDX	43.395	Sheet
Termite protection	1	Each
Building wrap	2248.78	SF
Water connection	1	Each

Doors

Quantity	Description	Type	Open R/L?
1	Door-b4068	RD05 Bifold	R
1	Door-b5068	RD05 Bifold	R
2	Door-e2868	RD01 Door ST	L
1	Door-e2868 glass	RD01 Door ST	L
1	Door-e3068 front	RD01 Door ST	R
1	Door-e5468 pair	RD02 Swing	L
2	Door-i1668	RD02 Swing	R
3	Door-12068	RD02 Swing	L
4	Door-i2068	RD02 Swing	R
1	Door-i2468	RD02 Swing	L
4	Door-i2668	RD02 Swing	R
1	Gar 8070	RD07 Overhead	L

Windows

Quantity	Description	Type
1	Wind-4040gl bk	W Glass Block 65
1	Wind-db5462	RW1-4 Doublehung
2	Wind-db6046	RW1-4 Doublehung
1	Wind-db6862	RW1-4 Doublehung
1	Wind-fixed2030	RW1-1 Stationary
5	Wind-s2062	RW1-4 Doublehung
2	Wind-s2442	RW1-4 Doublehung
4	Wind-s2446	RW1-4 Doublehung
1	Wind-s3046	RW1-4 Doublehung
1	Wind-s3462	RW1-1 Stationary

Electrical–Plumbing–Mechanical

Category	Descripton	Quantity	Unit
Electrical	Bath exhaust fan	3	Each
Electrical	Ceiling fan	2	Each
Electrical	Complete electric service, install	1	Each
Electrical	Outlet ceiling fixture	13	Each
Electrical	Outlet wall fixture	5	Each
Electrical	Receptacle 220v	1	Each
Electrical	Receptacle duplex outlet	36	Each
Electrical	Receptacle single outlet	1	Each
Electrical	Smoke detector, wired	1	Each
Electrical	Switch, 3-way	6	Each
Electrical	Switch, coupled	19	Each
Electrical	Telephone outlet	4	Each
Electrical	TV outlet	2	Each
Equipment	Dishwasher, medium	1	Each

Equipment	Free stand range/hood	1	Each
Equipment	Refrigerator, medium	1	Each
Plumbing	Bathtub	2	Each
Plumbing	Disposer, ½ hp	1	Each
Plumbing	HVAC equipment	1	Piece
Plumbing	Kitchen sink, dbl steel bowl	1	Each
Plumbing	Shower stall	1	Each
Plumbing	Vanity base, 1 sink	4	Each
Plumbing	Water closet, 2 piece, floor mounted	3	Each
Plumbing	Water heater	1	Piece

Index

D

F

Q–R

S